Fisher Investments on Industrials

FISHER INVESTMENTS PRESS

Fisher Investments Press brings the research, analysis, and market intelligence of Fisher Investments' research team, headed by CEO and *New York Times* best-selling author Ken Fisher, to all investors. The Press covers a range of investing and market-related topics for a wide audience—from novices to enthusiasts to professionals.

Books by Ken Fisher
The Ten Roads to Riches
The Only Three Questions That Count
100 Minds That Made the Market
The Wall Street Waltz
Super Stocks

Fisher Investments Series
Own the World
Aaron Anderson

20/20 Money
Michael Hanson

Fisher Investments On Series
Fisher Investments on Energy
Fisher Investments on Materials
Fisher Investments on Consumer Staples
Fisher Investments on Industrials

FISHER
INVESTMENTS
PRESS

Fisher Investments on Industrials

Fisher Investments
with
Matt Schrader and
Andrew S. Teufel

WILEY

John Wiley & Sons, Inc.

Published by John Wiley & Sons, Inc., Hoboken, New Jersey.

Published simultaneously in Canada.

For general information on our other products and services or for technical support, please contact our Customer Care Department within the United States at (800) 762-2974, outside the United States at (317) 572-3993 or fax (317) 572-4002.

Wiley also publishes its books in a variety of electronic formats. Some content that appears in print may not be available in electronic books. For more information about Wiley products, visit our web site at www.wiley.com.

Library of Congress Cataloging-in-Publication Data:

Fisher Investments.
    Fisher Investments on consumer staples / Fisher Investments with Michael Cannivet, Andrew S. Teufel.
        p.   cm. — (Fisher Investments Press)
    Includes bibliographical references and index.
    ISBN 978-0-470-41665-5 (pbk.)
        1. Consumer goods—United States—History.   2. Consumption (Economics)—United States—History.   I. Cannivet, Michael.   II. Teufel, Andrew S.   III. Title.
    HF1040.8.F56 2009
    332.67'22—dc22

                                                                                    2009001913

ISBN-13 978-0-470-45228-8

Printed in the United States of America

10 9 8 7 6 5 4 3 2 1

Contents

Foreword

Welcome to the fourth in a series of investing guides from Fisher Investments Press—the first ever imprint from a money manager, produced in partnership with John Wiley & Sons. This particular guide is on one category of stocks—Industrials—the most diverse of all the standard investing sectors. Those newer to investing will immediately think of heavy machinery and manufacturing—and maybe airplanes. But this broad sector also hits bridges and tunnels, defense, transportation services, and even light bulbs and package delivery.

Another interesting feature about Industrials: Industrials firms overwhelmingly have customers in other businesses and governments. They're not heavily retail-oriented—the way Health Care, Consumer Staples, or Consumer Discretionary firms are. Instead, these firms produce huge machinery or other complex products—with big sticker prices. And for this reason, out of all the sectors, Industrials has historically been among the most economically sensitive, and most correlated to the broader market. When you think about those big ticket items, it makes sense. If Machinery and Defense firms anticipate rough economic times, they're less likely to spend big money to update equipment. Which is why it's important to not only understand what drives Industrials, but also what drives their end-customers' spending plans. This book details what to look for.

But it's not as simple as anticipating economic cycles. Each industry has unique drivers. And because the life-cycle for many Industrials products can be long—regardless of the economy—and how long-term contracts are negotiated also plays a role, it's important to learn to anticipate where demand is coming from next. This book shows you how.

Manufacturing globally has been evolving tremendously over the past few decades, and continues to evolve. This book provides background on the modern production process—from lean manufacturing to Six Sigma—to help you understand how we got here and how it's likely to continue evolving. A significant theme is globalization and liberalization of trade policy, which helped give rise to the Asian Tigers (as detailed here)—and which will give rise to the next round of global tigers.

What this book doesn't provide is hot stock tips or a simple to-do list for picking the right stocks. Such a thing doesn't exist. Instead, this book, and all the books in the series, aims to give you a workable, top-down framework for analyzing a sector. The framework gives you tools allowing you to use commonly-available information to uncover profitable opportunities others overlook. And those opportunities should allow you to make market bets relative to an appropriate benchmark that win more often than lose. This isn't a framework that goes stale. Rather, this is a scientific method that should serve you all throughout your investing career. So good luck and enjoy the journey.

Ken Fisher
CEO of Fisher Investments
Author of the *New York Times*
Best Sellers *The Ten Roads to Riches* and
The Only Three Questions That Count

Preface

The *Fisher Investments On* series is designed to provide individual investors, students, and aspiring investment professionals the tools necessary to understand and analyze investment opportunities, primarily for investing in global stocks.

Within the framework of a "top-down" investment method (more on that in Chapter 7), each guide is an easily accessible primer to economic sectors, regions, or other components of the global stock market. While this guide is specifically on Industrials, the basic investment methodology is applicable for analyzing any global sector, regardless of the current macroeconomic environment.

Why a top-down method? Vast evidence shows high-level, or "macro," investment decisions are ultimately more important portfolio performance drivers than individual stocks. In other words, before picking stocks, investors can benefit greatly by first deciding if stocks are the best investment relative to other assets (like bonds or cash), and then choosing categories of stocks most likely to perform best on a forward-looking basis.

For example, a Technology sector stock picker in 1998 and 1999 probably saw his picks soar as investors cheered the so-called "New Economy." However, from 2000 to 2002, he probably lost his shirt. Was he just smarter in 1998 and 1999? Did his analysis turn bad somehow? Unlikely. What mattered most was stocks in general, and especially US technology stocks, did great in the late 1990s and poorly entering the new century. In other words, a top-down perspective on the broader economy was key to navigating markets—stock picking just wasn't as important.

Fisher Investments on Industrials will help guide you in making top-down investment decisions specifically for the Industrials sector. It shows how to determine better times to invest in Industrials, what Industrials industries and sub-industries are likelier to do best, and how individual stocks can benefit in various environments. The global Industrials sector is complex, covering many sub-industries and countries with unique characteristics. Using our framework, you will be better equipped to identify their differences, spot opportunities, and avoid major pitfalls.

This book takes a global approach to Industrials investing. Most US investors typically invest the majority of their assets in domestic securities; they forget America is less than half of the world stock market by weight—over 50 percent of investment opportunities are outside our borders. This is especially true in Industrials as many of the world's largest firms are based in foreign nations. Even domestic Industrials are relying more on manufacturing outside of the US and are deriving a significant portion of their profits overseas. Given the vast market landscape and diverse geographic operations, it's vital to have a global perspective when investing in Industrials today.

USING YOUR INDUSTRIALS GUIDE

This guide is designed in three parts. Part I, "Getting Started in Industrials," discusses vital sector basics and Industrials' high-level drivers. Here we'll discuss Industrials' main drivers—government and corporate spending—and explain how to capitalize on a wide array of macro conditions and industry-specific features to help you form an opinion on each of the industries within the sector. We'll also discuss additional drivers affecting the sector that ultimately drive Industrials' stock prices.

Part I also includes a discussion on the history of modern manufacturing since 1950 and what has shaped the world's current manufacturing landscape. Topics discussed include globalization, the rise of Asia, and the importance of manufacturing in the US today.

Part II, "Next Steps: Industrials Details," walks through the next step of sector analysis. We'll take you through the global Industrials sector investment universe and its diverse components. The Industrials sector is arguably the most diverse sector, which makes a thorough analysis challenging, but also increases your chances of finding successful investment opportunities and profitable segments of the market.

There are currently 14 industries within the Industrials sector. We will take you through the major components of the sector in detail, including a discussion on their end-markets, how they operate, and what drives profitability—to give you the tools to determine which industry will most likely outperform or underperform looking forward. Note: We spend less time on the Commercial Services & Supplies industry group, as it makes up a very small portion of the sector and the global stock market.

Part II also details where to find and how to interpret publicly available industry data. There are ample free resources, websites, and data sources to help in making better forward-looking sector, industry, and stock decisions.

Part II concludes with a discussion about the global infrastructure markets including the drivers and risks behind investment, the benefits to the Industrials sector, and ways to participate in the infrastructure boom.

Part III, "Thinking Like a Portfolio Manager," delves into a top-down investment methodology and individual security analysis. You'll learn to ask important questions like: What are the most important elements to consider when analyzing Machinery and Defense? What are the greatest risks and red flags? This book gives you a five-step process to help differentiate firms so you can identify ones with a greater probability of outperforming. We'll also discuss a few investment strategies to help determine when and how to overweight specific industries within the sector.

Note: We've specifically kept the strategies presented here high level so you can return to the book for guidance no matter the market conditions. But we also can't possibly address every market scenario and how markets may change over time. Many additional considerations should also be taken into account when crafting a portfolio strategy, including your own investing goals, your time horizon, and other factors unique to you. Therefore, you shouldn't rely solely on the strategies and pointers addressed here, as they won't always apply. Rather, this book is intended to provide general guidance and help you begin thinking critically not only about the Industrials sector, but about investing in general.

Further, *Fisher Investments on Industrials* won't give you a "silver bullet" for picking the right Industrials stocks. The fact is the "right" Industrials stocks will be different in different times and situations. Instead, this guide provides a framework for understanding the sector and its industries so that you can be dynamic and find information the market hasn't yet priced in. There won't be any stock recommendations, target prices, or even a suggestion whether now is a good time to be invested in the Industrials sector. The goal is to provide you with tools to make these decisions for yourself, now and in the future. Ultimately, our aim is to give you the framework for repeated, successful investing. Enjoy.

Acknowledgments

This book would not have been possible without the help, guidance, and support of many. To begin, we would like to thank Ken Fisher for providing us the resources and opportunity to write this book. We are also grateful to Jeff Silk for sharing his perspective and providing his guidance throughout the book-writing process.

Our great colleagues, editors, and designers proved vital in this process and deserve our sincerest praise for their hard work as well. In particular, Michael Hanson and Lara Hoffmans were instrumental in seeing this book through to completion. Their early guidance in the book's formation helped shaped the content and layout while their editing, advice, and support ultimately got us through to the finish line.

Fellow Industrials' analyst Patrick Hejlik made meaningful contributions to the book's content and was a great resource in the development of the book's ideas as well. We are thankful for his creativity and expertise. We applaud the hard work and help of Evelyn Chea and Dina Ezzat for their impressive attention to detail. We would also like to thank Scott Botterman for his great job creating the book's graphics and effectively presenting our ideas from mere concepts.

Of course Scott's ability to make such great graphics would only be possible with the help of our data vendors, to whom we owe a big thank you. We are grateful to Thomson Datastream, Thomson Reuters, Global Financial Data, and Standard & Poor's for allowing us to use their information. We'd also like to thank our team at Wiley for their support and guidance throughout this project, especially David Pugh and Kelly O'Connor.

Matt Schrader would also specifically like to thank his family for their constant support and encouragement through the book-writing process. Matt extends his heartfelt appreciation and love to Carl, Lisa, Enid, Grant, and Ben.

GETTING STARTED IN INDUSTRIALS

I

INDUSTRIALS BASICS

Mr. *Grant started his Sunday morning with some housework— taking out the trash, mowing the lawn, cleaning the pool, changing light bulbs, installing cabinets, and fixing the air conditioner.*

It was a productive day until 2:00 PM when his shoulder cushioned a fall off his ladder, requiring a trip to the ER. Making matters worse, Mr. Grant's normal route was getting re-paved, forcing him to take the long way through a $5 toll road to the hospital.

The bad news: He needed an MRI and a shoulder specialist—the closest was an hour's plane flight away.

Early Monday, he took the train to the airport and boarded a jet. At the hospital, he got his MRI, and the doctor told Mr. Grant his shoulder would be fine in time. Mr. Grant celebrated with a shopping spree through the airline's gift catalogue, fixing Post-it notes on everything he wanted to buy.

This is more than a simple anecdote with a happy ending—it's an illustration of the importance of Industrials products in our everyday lives. Every event, action, and item in Mr. Grant's travails used products and services, from the Industrials sector. Table 1.1 lists just some of the Industrials products and services Mr. Grant encountered.

Table 1.1   Industrials Sector Impact on Mr. Grant

Action	Industrials Sector Involvement
Taking out the trash	Pick-up service provided by a Commercial Services & Supplies company
Mowing the lawn	Lawnmower made by a Machinery company
Changing light bulbs	Light bulb manufactured by an Electrical Equipment company
Installing cabinets	Cabinets manufactured by a Building Products company
Fixing the air conditioner	Air conditioner manufactured by an Aerospace & Defense company
Road getting re-paved	Road paving equipment manufactured by a Machinery company
Paying $5 on the toll road	Toll road operated by a Transportation Infrastructure company
Taking the train to the airport	Train manufactured by a Machinery company and operated by a Road & Rail company
Taking the plane flight	Plane manufactured by an Aerospace & Defense company and operated by an Airline
Getting an MRI	MRI machine manufactured by an Industrial Conglomerate
Shopping from an airplane catalogue	Package delivery services provided by a Air Freight & Logistics company

The Industrials sector, arguably more than any other, is vastly diverse. Because it's not focused on a particular product or service, myriad drivers, end markets, and operating conditions can impact profitability of Industrials firms. And, while diverse, Industrials have played a very important role in global economic development. The sector has progressed globalization and global trade, it has built the world's infrastructure and boosted quality of life, and it has driven significant gains in productivity and manufacturing efficiency.

INDUSTRIALS BASICS

What does the Industrials sector look like from a high level? Because it has many diverse industries, it's split into three broad categories (as defined by the Global Industry Classification Standard [GICS] classification system). Firms in these categories primarily serve governments and corporations, but in some cases serve consumers as well:

- Capital Goods
- Transportation
- Commercial Services & Supplies

Capital Goods, the largest sector component, consists primarily of firms involved in production and making machinery and industrial goods including airplanes, tractors, power generators, and defense and transportation equipment. Globally, there are over 4,300 publicly traded Capital Goods firms.[1]

Transportation firms, the second largest weight within the sector, mostly ship goods rather than make them. Most forms of transportation are included in this group, including planes, trucks, ships, and railroads. Globally, there are nearly 900 publicly traded Transportation firms.[2]

Last, Commercial and Professional Services are a mixed bag, including commercial printing, data processing, environmental waste and garbage pickup, janitorial services, and staffing services. While seemingly disparate, these firms are generally service focused. Globally, there are over 1,000 publicly traded firms classified as Commercial and Professional Services.[3]

Industrials by the Numbers

The 200 largest Industrials companies employ over 11.5 million people globally—greater than the populations of Greece, Sweden, Switzerland, Hong Kong, Israel, or Denmark.

These firms generated over $3.1 trillion in revenues in 2007—larger than the size of the entire economy of every country in the world except the US, Japan, Germany, and China. And they had over $5.1 trillion worth of assets—more than the value of all durable goods (goods meant to last more than three years) owned by US households and nonprofit organizations.

Source: Bloomberg Finance L.P.; CIA 2008 World Fact Book; US Federal Reserve; IMF World Economic Outlook Database.

Table 1.2   World's Largest Industrials Companies as of 12/31/08

Name	US Ticker	Country	Industry	Market Value
General Electric	GE	US	Industrial Conglomerates	$161,278
Siemens	SI	Germany	Industrial Conglomerates	$67,087
United Technologies	UTX	US	Aerospace & Defense	$50,953
3M	MMM	US	Industrial Conglomerates	$39,873
United Parcel Services	UPS	US	Air Freight & Logistics	$37,372
ABB	ABB	Switzerland	Electrical Equipment	$34,000
Lockheed Martin	LMT	US	Aerospace & Defense	$33,683
Boeing	BA	US	Aerospace & Defense	$31,270
East Japan Railway	EJPRY	Japan	Road & Rail	$30,403
Emerson Electric	EMR	US	Electrical Equipment	$28,082

Source: Thomson Datastream.

Industrials Leaders

Industrials firms can play a vital role in the global economy because of the functions they serve, the markets they affect, and the scope and scale of their operations. But who are these firms? Table 1.2 shows the world's largest Industrials firms (by market cap). GE, one of the world's largest firms, nearly triples the size of the next biggest. Seven of the ten largest are US-domiciled, but they vary greatly by industry. And all operate in multiple markets and industries, producing goods ranging from Post-it notes to power generation equipment.

Over time, these firms have grown via mergers, product extensions, and growth into new markets—the result being significant economies of scale, highly recognizable brand names, and global diversification. These firms are generally considered industry "bellwethers" and are good firms to analyze to understand their industries.

INDUSTRIALS CHARACTERISTICS

There's no denying Industrials firms can be massive with a broad scale of operations. And while they are a diverse group, they do have a few more unifying characteristics and attributes. Generally, the Industrials sector as a whole:

- Is diverse—both in where the firms are domiciled and in the end markets scrved,
- Tends to be economically sensitive,
- Is highly correlated to broad markets, and
- Tends to have lower profit margins.

Let's look at each of these characteristics in a bit more detail.

A Diverse World

The Industrials sector is diverse—including where they're domiciled and the end markets served. These firms manufacture equipment and provide services—factory equipment, machinery, and transportation and supply chain services, to name a few—to a wide range of other sectors and government branches. Most manufacturing industries—from food production to car manufacturing—require production equipment that is often produced by an Industrials firm. These equipment manufacturers fall into a select number of industries (whether in Industrials or another sector), but the number of industries and end markets served is significantly more.

Freight transportation firms are responsible for shipping other industries' products globally, giving these industries exposure to multiple drivers and providing them with significant diversification. For example, railroads generate revenue from myriad markets like food, clothing, coal, lumber, motor vehicles, and metals.

Unlike most sectors, Industrials industries are not always cohesively linked. It's easy to see why oil exploration firms might be classified in the same sector as an oil refiner, but the link isn't as clear among a machinery producer, a staffing firm, and a railroad—all classified as Industrials.

Larger Industrials firms serve regionally diverse end markets as well. In some cases, firms have a greater portion of foreign sales than domestic. Among other factors, improved technology and communication abilities, increased globalization, and the liberalization of trade, investment, and the financial markets have driven significant changes in revenue distribution and the potential to penetrate foreign markets. Table 1.3 highlights a few firms whose revenue distribution has changed significantly in just 15 years. While not every firm's gains are as remarkable as these, greater regional diversification is common for many Industrials. And with this diversification comes a host of new market opportunities and the ability to access new and potentially cheaper labor and suppliers.

This diversification is not solely a US phenomenon either as many non-US firms share similar changes in revenue distribution. The ability and the need to focus globally to grow—whether through new joint ventures, mergers, investment in distribution channels, or other initiatives—has enhanced the competitive landscape of the Industrials sector. New, smaller regional players have also increased their market presence, driving increased competition as well.

Economically Sensitive

Another commonality is Industrials are generally considered economically sensitive. Firms tend to buy new equipment or ship more goods when the economy is strong, profitability is rising, and future market

Table 1.3   Percent of Foreign Revenues for Leading US Industrials Firms (1992–2007)

Company	1992	2007	Difference
Paccar	21%	64%	43%
General Electric	17%	51%	34%
3M	43%	63%	20%
Emerson Electric	33%	52%	19%
United Technologies	40%	51%	11%

Source: SEC, Standard & Poor's Research Insight.

expectations are positive. Industrials are generally driven by broad macro factors—corporate profitability, access to credit, increased spending, and so on—all of which are positive drivers for the economy as a whole. As a result, Industrials tend to move in cycles closely aligned with the broader economy and the end markets served (which are often cyclical industries themselves).

Industrials tend to manufacture and provide services for expensive big-ticket items that can typically run for years. This can increase sales volatility as firms tend to delay making expensive purchases when times are tough. (Note, firms do generate a portion of revenues from selling spare parts and service, which is more stable.) Contrast this with a sector like Consumer Staples where demand can be fairly constant. For example, demand for food isn't as economically sensitive as that for a mining truck.

Industrials' economic sensitivity is exhibited in Figure 1.1, comparing Industrials' annual sales growth as a whole, as well as the Transportation and Capital Goods industry groups (left axis), to

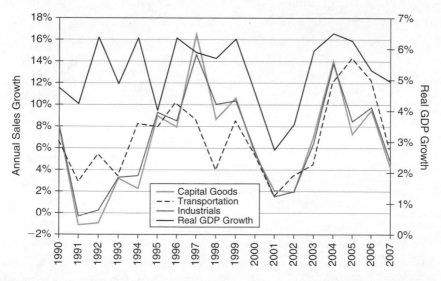

Figure 1.1   S&P 500 Industrials Sector Sales Growth vs. GDP Growth

Source: Standard & Poor's and Bloomberg Finance L.P.

the annual US GDP growth (right axis) from 1990 through 2007. While the magnitude of growth and the rate of change are greater for Industrials than the overall economy, the overall direction and inflection points are generally similar.

Why does economic sensitivity matter? The sector's leverage to the economy and a diverse set of drivers can allow it to disproportionately benefit when economic conditions are generally good. For example, look at Figure 1.1 again—when GDP growth hit 5.9 percent in 1997, Industrials' sales growth was nearly 15 percent.

Industrials can benefit from many facets of economic growth—increased manufacturing, increased construction, increased corporate, consumer, and government spending, etc. For this reason, many of the larger Industrials firms—FedEx, UPS, General Electric, United Technologies, and Union Pacific, to name a few—are generally considered good barometers for the US economy.

But volatile product demand can lead to operational challenges, market uncertainty, and increased business risks, like the following:

- **Forecasting challenges**. Volatile demand can make capital budgeting decisions, project profitability expectations, and growth estimates a challenge.
- **Ill-conceived production changes**. Expanding production can prove problematic and be a poor use of capital. Conversely, not producing enough leaves profits on the table and may lead to competitors taking market share.
- **Excess inventory issues**. No firm wants to be left with excess inventories when economic growth and product demand fade. There is money tied up in inventory, and product price reductions may become necessary.

From an investor's standpoint, the challenge is forecasting sales and earnings in consideration of ever-changing market conditions and how effective management will be in countering such operational challenges. What might be true today may not be true in a year. This is one reason Industrials tends to have lower valuations than other sectors.

High Correlation to Broad Markets

Economic sensitivity is one reason Industrials tend to be strongly correlated to broader markets. Industrials historically have the highest correlation of any sector to the S&P 500 and very near the highest correlation to the MSCI World (a global stock market index). Table 1.4 shows the monthly correlation between the S&P 500 and the MSCI World for standard investing sectors from 1995 through 2008. During this period, Industrials had a 0.9 correlation to both the US and the world stock markets.

Note that two of the most economically sensitive sectors— Industrials and Consumer Discretionary—have among the highest correlations, while sectors considered less economically sensitive— Health Care and Consumer Staples—rank among the lowest.

Industrials are also more closely correlated to the stock market overall than any individual sector. Table 1.5 shows the correlation of the S&P 500 Industrials and MSCI World Industrials sectors to the remaining nine sectors and each aggregate index. For example, both the S&P 500 Industrials and the MSCI World Industrials have a 0.9

Table 1.4   Sector Correlations to the S&P 500 and the MSCI World (1995–2008)

Sector	Correlation to the S&P 500	Correlation to the MSCI World
Industrials	0.9	0.9
Consumer Discretionary	0.9	0.9
Technology	0.8	0.8
Financials	0.8	0.9
Materials	0.7	0.8
Telecom Services	0.7	0.7
Health Care	0.6	0.6
Energy	0.5	0.6
Consumer Staples	0.5	0.6
Utilities	0.4	0.7

Source: Thomson Datastream.

Table 1.5   Industrials Sector Correlations to the S&P 500 and the MSCI World Sectors (1995–2008)

Sector	Correlation to the S&P 500 Industrials	Correlation to the MSCI World Industrials
Index (S&P 500/MSCI World)	0.9	0.9
Consumer Discretionary	0.8	0.9
Materials	0.8	0.9
Financials	0.8	0.8
Technology	0.7	0.7
Consumer Staples	0.5	0.6
Energy	0.5	0.6
Telecom Services	0.5	0.6
Health Care	0.5	0.5
Utilities	0.4	0.6

Source: Thomson DataStream.

correlation to the S&P 500 and MSCI World, respectively. This is much greater than the 0.5 correlation the Industrials sector has to the Health Care sector, both domestically and globally.

Lower Profit Margins

Another unifying factor among Industrials firms is their lower profit margins. This is partly due to the sector's sensitivity to raw materials used in production (copper, steel, aluminum, etc., for Capital Goods and oil for Transportation). For example, AMR Corp, the owner of American Airlines, spent over $9 billion in fuel in 2008, equal to roughly 35 percent of operating expenses (the firm's largest operating expense).[4] This sensitivity can significantly impact profits.

Table 1.6 shows historic average operating margins for S&P 500 firms by sector. As you can see, the Industrials sector is well below average.

While Industrials firms tend to hedge their commodity needs (AMR Corp saved $380 million due to its hedges in 2008[5]), they can still be negatively exposed to input cost fluctuations and price increases by suppliers—more than the aggregate market.

Table 1.6 Average Operating Margin of S&P 500 Companies (2000–2007)

Sector	2000	2001	2002	2003	2004	2005	2006	2007	Average
Consumer Discretionary	9.6	8.6	10.1	11.1	12.0	12.0	11.7	10.6	10.7
Consumer Staples	12.6	12.9	13.5	13.6	13.4	13.2	13.3	13.4	13.2
Energy	17.7	21.1	12.9	15.9	18.4	22.7	27.4	26.3	20.3
Financials	25.2	23.5	25.3	28.1	29.1	28.6	29.2	33	27.8
Health Care	15.1	14.8	17.9	16.7	18.0	19.0	17.9	17.8	17.1
Industrials	12.5	10.9	11.1	10.4	11.2	12.1	12.8	12.8	11.7
Tech	−7.8	−20.7	−0.4	9.3	14.9	16.8	16.2	15.0	5.4
Materials	11.9	9.8	9.9	10	12.0	14.0	15.1	13.7	12.1
Telecom	9.9	6.6	14	14.9	16.6	20.2	20.6	21.8	16.0
Utilities	16.9	19.1	17.8	14.7	15.5	13.5	15.9	16	16.2
Total	**12.3**	**10.0**	**13.3**	**15.3**	**17.0**	**17.7**	**18.2**	**18.4**	**15.3**

Source: Bloomberg Finance L.P.

THE MODERN PRODUCTION PROCESS

Because the largest Industrials industries (by market capitalization) are manufacturing related, no understanding of the overall sector would be complete without an overview of the modern production process. Operationally, the supply chain and the production process are crucial because they dictate quality and quantity of goods produced, drive profitability and margin improvements, and can drive competitive advantages over peers. Therefore, these firms dedicate much capital to, and focus on, improving production abilities.

Two of the most important developments in the modern production process have been the revolution toward *lean manufacturing* and broad adaptation of *Six Sigma*—two fairly widely used business strategies. These strategies were born out of discontent with the ineffectiveness of mass production in today's fast-changing and quality-driven world.

But this does not diminish the importance of mass production in the early twentieth century and how it revolutionized manufacturing and drove substantial productivity gains. The system, made popular by auto maker Henry Ford, capitalized on production economies of scale by using simple-to-attach, interchangeable parts for assembly line production.

In 1908, the average task cycle—the amount of time it took a laborer to perform a task on a new car—was 514 minutes. By 1913, after the introduction of a moving assembly line, the cycle had decreased to 1.19 minutes. Ford's cars were cheaper to produce, quicker to manufacture, and easier to fix than competitors. Rivals and other manufacturing industries took note and, by the mid-twentieth century, mass production was standard in the US and Europe.[6]

While mass production proved successful, by the 1950s, flaws in the system began emerging. Sleek new European car designs began stealing market share from American producers, and competition from Japan began accentuating mass production flaws—including the incentive to let defective cars reach final assembly, and the cost and waste of excess inventories.

Because changing production lines was expensive, US manufacturers were ill-prepared to deal with evolving consumer demand, the

When Good Technology Goes Bad

By the 1980s, the US began investing in new technologies to improve productivity and increase efficiency. Unfortunately for some, the learning curve was steep and mastering the technology proved challenging. Automotive analyst and author Maryann Keller saw these challenges firsthand in 1985 when she visited a new Cadillac manufacturing plant in Michigan. She discovered out-of-control robots spray painting each other, destroying windshields, and smashing into themselves and other cars.

Thankfully, US manufacturers got better using robots as time progressed and by 2009 there were over an estimated 186,000 robots used in the US (second only to Japan) and over one million used globally.

Source: John Teresko, "It Came From Japan!" *IndustryWeek* (February 1, 2005); Robotics Industries Association.

increasing importance of reliability, and auto-industry fragmentation. And while these attributes were detrimental for US manufacturers, they highlighted the strengths of the new Japanese system—more malleable, flexible, and cooperative production. The result was the birth of lean manufacturing, the Toyota Production System, and Japanese car manufacturers' rise to prominence.

Lean manufacturing

At its core, lean manufacturing aims to improve overall profitability by eliminating waste through reduction of production inputs and limiting excess production. Done right, this reduces costs and working capital, improves quality, shortens manufacturing time, and creates production flexibility.

Lean manufacturing has resulted in a number of benefits over mass production, including the following productivity gains:

- **Reduced Time.** Engineering, product development, and design take half the time.
- **Reduced Human Effort.** The same production output requires half the human effort.
- **Reduced Space.** Floor space required reduced by half.

- **Reduced WIP.** Work-in-process inventory (WIP) reduced by nine-tenths.
- **Reduced Processing Time.** Processing time reduced by nine-tenths.[7]

Elimination of Waste   One of the most important ways lean manufacturing is able to accomplish these gains is by eliminating excess waste and unnecessary inventory and supplies. Waste elimination—whether inputs or outputs—can significantly reduce costs and improve profit margins. Not only is inventory expensive, it takes up room, is a distraction to workers and production, and can be rendered useless with product design changes.

The risk of product defects with large inventories increases as well. Under mass production, large batches of inventory were produced at the same time. If something went awry during production, it increased the likelihood all the components had the same issue. And if there was excess inventory, the problem might not have been discovered and rectified until much later—all while faulty products continued making their way to market.

To counter these risks, manufacturers have changed their relationships with suppliers—shifting to more frequent, smaller deliveries rather than large shipments. Thanks to improvements in transportation and the realignment of production, firms can increasingly deliver necessary components with shorter lead times, creating a more constant flow of production and inventory.

Lean manufacturing can also improve manufacturing flow. Today, factories can have more consistent flow, minimizing extra parts and inventories to eliminate waste, including unnecessary removal time. Production bottlenecks and issues can be greatly eliminated once they're recognized and manufacturing activity is constantly flowing.

Rather than produce goods *expected* to be in demand, lean manufacturers strive to produce only what is *needed* to meet current demand. This can reduce a major waste—overcapacity—and in the process, free up capital, limit unnecessary component purchases, and lessen the chance of having to reduce product prices. It also gives a manufacturer the flexibility of shifting production levels without creating excess inventories.

The result has been a marked improvement in total inventory held relative to total sales and overall production efficiency. Figure 1.2 shows the inventories to sales ratio for US manufacturers from 1967 through 2007. Outside of spikes in the early 1980s, the ratio has trended down over the period. Reduced inventory has mitigated some of the harm of falling demand while freeing up capital, space, and time.

Six Sigma The increased importance on product reliability and quality has also led US manufacturers to try a host of other manufacturing techniques ranging from Total Quality Management (TQM), Just-in-Time Manufacturing (JIT), Statistical Process Control (SPC), and other international manufacturing techniques. But of these systems, Motorola's Six Sigma has arguably become the most popular.

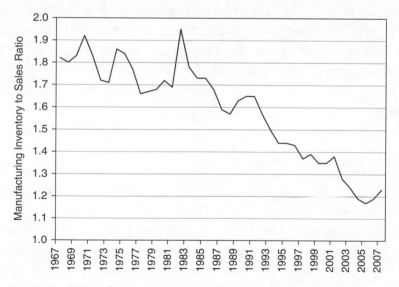

Figure 1.2   Manufacturing Inventories to Sales Ratio
Source: US Census Bureau.

Lean Manufacturing at Work

The Defense industry learned firsthand the benefits of lean manufacturing and modern production techniques. In an effort to cut costs and boost competitiveness against growing rivals, US defense contractor Boeing began implementing modern manufacturing techniques in the late 1990s and within years had doubled production of its C-17 military plane, helping the Pentagon save hundreds of millions of dollars.

Source: Andrew Pollack, "Aerospace Gets Japan's Message; Without Military Largess, Industry Takes the Lean Path," *The New York Times* (March 9, 1999).

Six Sigma aims to improve product quality and enhance customer value by eliminating production defects. By defining production issues and goals, and establishing data to analyze improvements, a firm can better determine the magnitude of a problem, anticipate the effectiveness of a proposed solution, and control future process performance. A major goal for a Six Sigma firm is removing variation. The smaller the spread between expected and actual production, the greater the flexibility a firm has in producing a good. An efficient firm whose manufacturing time only varies by a day has greater flexibility in determining when to start production over a firm whose production time varies by a week. The reduction of variation allows more predictable business processes and increases the chance of accomplishing the most important goal—pleasing the customer.

Specifically, under the Six Sigma production strategy, the ultimate goal is to reduce defects (anything not meeting customer requirements) to no more than 3.4 per million opportunities (an opportunity is any chance a defect could arise). While ambitious, the program's savings has justified the effort. Between 1987 and 2005, 53 percent of Fortune 500 companies used Six Sigma and claimed an estimated $427 billion savings using the system.[8]

Six Sigma has been an important part of the success of many Industrials firms such as Honeywell, General Electric, Raytheon, Caterpillar, FedEx, 3M, Northrop Grumman, Ingersoll Rand, and Tyco International. The gains for many have been substantial. Honeywell (previously Allied Signal) initiated Six Sigma in 1992 and by 1999 was saving more than $600 million a year in costs.[9] For General Electric, the benefit reached over $2 billion by 1999.[10]

The impact of these programs goes beyond simple cost savings. Customers will often pay more money for higher quality machines with higher productivity and fewer breakdowns and maintenance requirements. For many, the marginal cost increase of a relatively pricier capital good is less than the potential opportunity costs associated with machinery breakdowns. As a result, Six Sigma firms with higher product quality may also find they can charge higher prices and have greater brand loyalty.

Chapter Recap

This chapter introduced fundamental characteristics distinguishing the Industrials sector and how it operates. Later chapters will build on these concepts, including:

- The sector is composed of three main segments—Capital Goods, Transportation, and Commercial Services & Supplies.
- Industrials firms are typically highly diverse, economically sensitive, highly correlated to the market, and have lower-than-average profit margins.
- Mass production has given way to new production techniques, like lean manufacturing and Six Sigma, which have improved quality, efficiency, and production costs

2

HISTORY OF MODERN MANUFACTURING

The Industrials sector has a rich and diverse history, ranging from the epic building of the cross-continental railroads to the sea change in world economic development—the Industrial Revolution—and even played a vital role in the World Wars. But as revolutionary as those early events were, we've witnessed yet another revolution in Industrials' development since World War II.

Among the most significant post-war trends is globalization. Liberalization of financial markets and increased openness of trade have driven foreign investment, while improvements in transportation, technology, and the ability to outsource production have enabled multinational firms to manufacture and compete globally. The result has been a change from manufacturing primacy of the UK and US to Asia, including Japan, Hong Kong, China, Singapore, Taiwan, and South Korea. US manufacturing still plays an important role in global manufacturing and in the US economy, but its impact has lessened relatively.

THE ADVANCEMENT OF TRADE AND INVESTMENT

One of the most important economic changes since World War II has been increased global integration and its impact on world manufacturing and multinational corporations. This is particularly true for Industrials because of its global diversification and production focus. Market liberalization and globalization have not only allowed for greater foreign product competitiveness and sales, but have enabled imports of cheaper parts and components used in final production in the US as well.

Evidence of Globalization

While the benefits and beneficiaries of globalization have long been disputed, no one refutes that changes—often substantial—are evident. Increases in global trade, growing foreign direct investment (FDI), and increased cross border merger activity highlight the magnitude of growing global connectedness and integration.

Global Trade   The acceleration of world trade is among the most notable developments. Figure 2.1 shows growth in merchandise trade (sum of all exports and imports globally minus goods en route to a different country) as a percent of gross domestic product (GDP) since 1960. From 1960 through 2007, the total value of merchandise trade as a percent of GDP rose from 22 percent to 51 percent.

Many factors have contributed to this growth, including reduced trade barriers, improved developing nations' technical abilities, and the general propensity to shift manufacturing to countries with cheaper production costs. In recent years, large infrastructure projects and increased global economic growth have driven substantial commodity demand increases and merchandise trade as well.

Foreign Direct Investment   Increased global economic integration is also evident in global fixed-asset investment. FDI represents investment in foreign buildings, machines, equipment, and so on. This differs from indirect foreign investment—like the purchase of foreign stocks. Note the large run-up of FDI in Figure 2.2 during the 1990s when the global economy and stock market were strong, followed by a

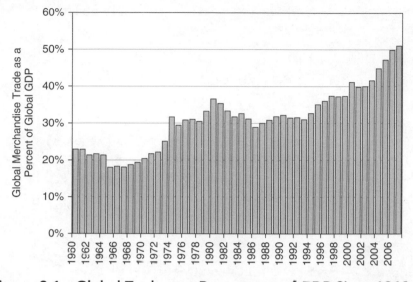

Figure 2.1   Global Trade as a Percentage of GDP Since 1960
Source: World Bank.

contraction during the 2000 to 2002 bear market, and ultimate resurgence in investment once the global economy and markets recovered. By 2007, FDI hit record highs of $1.25 trillion in the developed world and $1.8 trillion globally.

Also impactful is the growing portion of fixed assets funded by foreign investment. Through the mid-1990s, FDI accounted for less than 5 percent of total fixed-asset investment globally and in developed economies. But as investment accelerated, FDI's share of total fixed assets boomed, reaching over 20 percent in developed countries in 2000. While markets fell dramatically during the subsequent bear market, the share increased afterward and by 2007 was near 16 percent.

The use of these fixed-asset facilities has been mixed—in some instances, these structures are simply used as a production facility, while in others, they're used to establish a local market presence and sales base. For example, US machinery producer Caterpillar uses its presence in China to do both—it has 11 Chinese manufacturing facilities and uses them to boost component production as well as a base to sell to Asian customers.

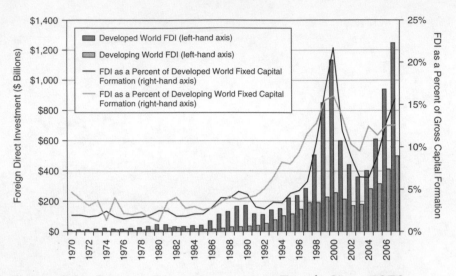

Figure 2.2   Foreign Direct Investment Trends Since 1970
Source: United Nations.

Factory construction also increases the investor's exposure to the local market, which can lead to a host of secondary benefits like access to raw materials, new local suppliers, and highly skilled labor. The result is often improved geographic diversification and access to cheaper and/or more qualified labor. As Jack Welch, GE's former CEO, noted in the firm's 2000 Annual Report, "Globalization has transformed a heavily US-based Company to one whose revenues are now 40 percent non-US. Even more importantly, it has changed us into a Company that searches the world, not just to sell or to source, but to find intellectual capital: the world's best talent and greatest ideas."[1] By 2007, over 50 percent of the firm's revenue came from outside the US.[2]

For host nations, new investment ushers in valuable sources of new funding, new technologies, and skill development. Often, new investment goes to special economic zones (SEZ), where rules and regulations are typically relatively investor-friendly. Benefits to investing in these areas have included exemptions on duties and regulations, lessened tariffs on imported machines and raw materials, favorable tax rates, and land provisions. (More on SEZs a bit later.)

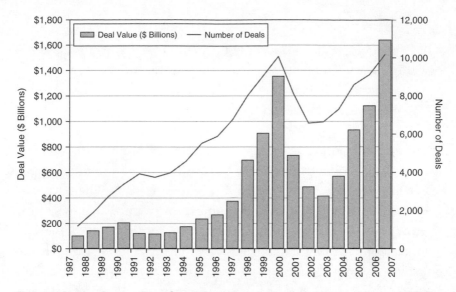

Figure 2.3   Cross-Border Mergers & Acquisitions Since 1987
Source: United Nations.

Cross-border Mergers and Acquisitions   Cross-border mergers and acquisition activity—deals involving buying or merging with a company from another country—has followed a similar trajectory as FDI. Figure 2.3 shows global cross-border mergers and acquisitions by number and deal value from 1987 through 2007.

Easing regulatory hurdles surrounding foreign company mergers has made entering new markets much easier for multinational firms. Similar to the benefits of foreign direct investment, a cross-border merger allows a multinational firm to establish a local base, increase brand awareness overseas, access new sales and distribution channels, and provide a greater source of foreign revenues. For example, South Korean machinery producer Doosan Infracore purchased America's Ingersoll-Rand's Bobcat division in 2007 for $4.9 billion. The deal gave Doosan Infracore a strong local brand name, new manufacturing technologies to incorporate into its other products, new sales distributors for other products, and new component suppliers for which to source parts. Sometimes it's easier to obtain these attributes through purchasing a firm rather than trying to build them from the ground up.

Globalization's Causes

What's behind the globalization trend? Among many factors, techno-logical improvements, improved transportation, improved trade relations, and multinational global focus are among the most significant causes of this international boom.

Technological Improvements Technological improvements dra-matically spurred globalization by decreasing the cost and expanding access to information and means of communication. The advent of cheap, effective, and reliable communication enabled manufacturing to move anywhere in the world but still be within direct communi-cation and monitoring. This allowed supply chains to be managed globally and more effectively and reduced production challenges. The development and gradual reduction in costs of telephones, wireless communication, computers, and the Internet have all played a role.

The cost of these technologies and the progression of globaliza-tion go hand in hand. For example, globalization has spurred new production in China and reduced manufacturing costs, which in turn spurs globalization as technologies and global expansions become cheaper.

Optimal Production and Increased Profits the Komatsu Way

Japanese heavy machinery manufacturer Komatsu uses a system called Standard Variable Management (SVM), which, through a series of computer calculations, enables the company to know exactly which of its factories a customer's order should ship from. The system has optimized production and led to financially sound decisions with the company being fully able to capitalize on the benefits of its global production base. As Komatsu Chairman Masahiro Sakane noted, "SVM makes a big difference in how fast we can adjust sales, production, and inventory control in response to demand fluctua-tions by region and model."

Source: Nikkei Net Interactive.

Improved Transportation   Improved transportation has also been integral to globalization. The efficiency, availability, and cost effectiveness of marine, rail, truck, and air transportation have made operating globally financially viable. And as global trade has increased, Industrials have responded by producing larger transportation equipment, creating larger and more sophisticated trading ports, offering more service-friendly freight options, and creating faster and more efficient air transport services.

The introduction of *containerzation* in the 1950s was a major step in the improvement of global transportation. Containerization refers to the shift from shipping goods via small bags and barrels to using large shipping containers and trailers. The large, standardized containers provide a number of advantages over more traditional methods, including:

- **Standardization.** Standardized containers, which are typically stacked up to seven high on container ships, allow for easy transfer of goods from one mode of transportation to another (called *intermodal transportation*), like ship to rail or rail to truck, as the containers can easily be lifted and moved.
- **Efficiency.** Moving containers with cranes is more efficient than "break-bulk" handing—moving barrels and containers individually. The result is increased economies of scale, lower costs, substantial time savings, and far less labor requirements.
- **Looting.** The reduction in dock times and the difficulty in manually handling one of the large containers lessened the amount of pilfering, which had been a major problem of globalized trade.
- **Reduced damage.** Large containers protected goods from damage much better than sticking them loosely in a ship's hull.

The advent of double-stacking technology (the ability to stack two containers on top of each other) for the railroads in the 1980s decreased shipping costs, increased shipping speeds, and enabled railroads to compete more effectively against trucking in freight shipping.

The advent of standardized shipping vessels and the subsequent rise of intermodal transportation (shipping via more than one mode of transportation) have also driven greater cooperation between marine, rail, and road freight transportation. It's not uncommon for goods today to be manufactured in Asia, transported via ship across the ocean, shipped across the country by rail, and later hauled to their final destination by truck—reducing overall shipping costs.

Trade Liberalization   Improved trade relations have created closer economic links between nations. One organization that has helped spur cooperation is the World Trade Organiation (WTO; and its predecessor General Agreement on Tariffs and Trade [GATT]), which provides a platform for handling trade disputes and an avenue to collectively compromise on tariffs. The group's efforts have been generally successful, with negotiations often leading to billions in savings for exporters, as seen in Table 2.1. Table 2.1 summarizes the outcomes of the WTO's trade negotiations from 1950 through 2001. Note increases in the number of nations and the reduction in tariffs as time progresses.

Reduction in tariffs and the removal of trade barriers fostered greater global competition and opened new market opportunities for exporters. The WTO grew from 15 countries in 1948 to 153 countries by 2008 and helped global trade increase 27-fold from 1950 through 2006—three times more than the global economic output during this period.[3]

The Rise of Multinational Corporations   Multinational firms played a big role in globalization's spread. These firms, with the capital, technology, and production capabilities necessary to operate globally, have acted as globalization's agents. They've capitalized on liberalized financial and trade markets through increased foreign direct investment, increased cross-border mergers and acquisitions, increased use of foreign affiliates, and more joint ventures. Higher energy costs, the ability to source goods locally, and increased foreign product demand have also led to decentralization of manufacturing.

Table 2.1   WTO Key Event Summary

Name of Trade Talk	Year	Countries/Parties	Weighted Tariff Reduction
Torquay	1951	38	8,700 tariff concessions, 1948 tariff levels cut by 25%
Geneva	1956	26	$2.5 billion in tariff reductions
Geneva (Dillon Round)	1960–1961	26	Tariff concessions worth $4.9 billion
Geneva (Kennedy Round)	1964–1967	62	Average tariffs reduced by 35%, cuts worth $40 billion
Geneva (Tokyo Round)	1973–1979	102	Tariff reductions worth more than $300 billion, average tariff reduced by 1/3 to 6% for OECD manufactures imports
Geneva (Uruguay Round)	1986–1994	123	Creation of the WTO, average tariff reduced by one-third
Doha	2001–	153	Not concluded

Source: BBC and the World Trade Organization.

As a result, it's common to see large multinational firms with more production bases in foreign markets than at home. Ingersoll Rand and Emerson Electric, two large US Industrials multinationals, both have over 50 percent of their manufacturing bases located outside the US as of September 2008.[4] According to the United Nations Conference on Trade and Development (UNCTAD), there were over 61,000 transnational corporations in 2002 producing goods in over 900,000 foreign affiliaties.[5] The size and scale of operations is concentrated at the top. The largest 100 multinational firms accounted for 14 percent of foreign affiliate sales worldwide, 12 percent of total assets, and 13 percent of total employment.[6]

THE RISE OF ASIA AND CHANGES IN THE MANUFACTURING LANDSCAPE

Among globalization's largest beneficiaries is Asia, which saw its share in total world merchandise exports nearly double between 1948 and

Table 2.2   World Merchandise Exports by Region

Country	1948	1963	1973	1983	1993	2005
US	22%	15%	12%	11%	13%	9%
UK	11%	8%	5%	5%	5%	4%
Germany*	1%	9%	12%	9%	10%	10%
China	1%	1%	1%	1%	3%	8%
Japan	0%	4%	6%	8%	10%	6%
Europe	35%	48%	51%	44%	45%	43%
North America	28%	20%	17%	17%	18%	15%
Asia	14%	13%	15%	19%	26%	27%
East Asian Tigers**	3%	2%	3%	6%	10%	10%

*Refers to the Federal Republic of Germany from 1948 through 1983.
**Includes Hong Kong, China, Malaysia, South Korea, Singapore, Taipei, and Thailand.

Source: World Trade Organization 2007 World Trade Report.

2005. Table 2.2 highlights the change in merchandise export growth from the end of World War II to 2005, during which period the share of US and UK global exports has consistently fallen.

To understand how and why so many Asian nations now compete globally, one must first understand the policies that spurred this growth historically. What was initially cultivated in Japan soon moved to the Asian Tigers (Singapore, South Korea, Hong Kong, and Taiwan), and later, China. The following pages document these changes and the source of their growth.

Japan's Rise

Like Europe, Japan was ravaged by World War II. In 1946, manufacturing output was only 30 percent of its pre-war highs, and its political and economic structure had been largely destroyed.[7] But Japan surprised the world with its industriousness, and its economy recovered, growing 10 percent per year through the 1950s and 1960s. Within five years of the war's end, Japan had become the world's third largest economy.

Manufacturing mirrored this increase, with production reaching pre-war highs by 1956 and manufacturing growth averaging 16 percent a year between 1950 and 1970.[8] For good reason, this period in Japanese history has been called the "economic miracle."

Big Government Takes Charge One of the major drivers of Japan's success was the government's pro-growth initiatives aimed at reinvigorating the economy after the war. The government, through a series of legislation and reassertions of power, re-focused Japan on advanced technology and heavy capital investment industries like steel, petrochemicals, ships, electronic goods, televisions, and later, automobiles. The success of these initiatives in the 1960s is evidenced in their growth—steel production grew by over 300 percent, television production increased over 280 percent, and automobile production increased over 18 times in the 1960s.[9]

The Japanese government provided a number of financial incentives to encourage exports and investment, including:

- **Tax shelters and write-offs.** The government provided favorable tax policies for certain industries, including tax incentives on export earnings, various tax write-offs, and accelerated depreciation on new equipment purchases.
- **Import control.** The government controlled imports, which in their view lessened foreign competition and helped fledgling industries grow.
- **Subsidized loans.** Preferential loan rates were given to favored industries, reducing the cost of investment.
- **Infrastructure spending.** The money spent on infrastructure grew by an average of 22 percent annually between 1955 and 1973 to fund creation of railways, airports, dams, and roads,[10] resulting in improved transportation systems, reduced manufacturing costs, and greater efficiency.

The "Keiretsu" Drives Bank and Manufacturer Cooperation
Unlike the US, the Japanese government actively encouraged long-term cooperation between firms and banks. Japanese firms after

World War II established the *horizontal keiretsu*—a series of interlocking firms similar to Industrial Conglomerates today. At the center of these groups was a bank responsible for loaning money to its member firms from various industries. (The Mitsubishi keiretsu controlled, among other businesses, a heavy machinery company, a trading house, an insurance company, and a brewery.)

The keiretsu group each took shares in its partnered firms, virtually eliminating the chance of a corporate takeover and fostering cooperation among member firms. And because the banks provided stable credit at favorable rates, firms could focus on increasing long-term profitability, foreign market penetration, and product quality rather than focus on shareholder short-term profit goals.[11]

Vertical keiretsu were also established with a major manufacturer at their core and their suppliers working closely alongside. The major firm in the center often held shares in its suppliers and remained a loyal customer in exchange for supplier assurance of cost and quality control and timely supplies, among other things. These relationships improved product quality and lowered costs, subsequently driving increased product competitiveness overseas.

Focus on Technology and Changes in Exports   The Japanese government also played an important role in promoting technology and competitiveness. By financing the purchase of technology from abroad, the government controlled both the foreign technologies purchased and who could buy them. The government often negotiated contracts itself, making it frequently cheaper to purchase than to develop technology.

More than one firm would typically buy this foreign technology as well, which encouraged efficiency by increasing competition. The result for Japan was improved technology and equipment at a fraction of the development time and cost.[12]

Later efforts were aided by improvements in manufacturing techniques, like the implementation of the "Toyota Production System" and use of factory automation equipment. Industrial robots became common, performing automated tasks like attaching car doors quickly and cheaply.

The Toyota Production System

Among the most famous examples of technology and innovation success in Japan has been the *Toyota Production System*. The system is centered on two principles—automation and inventory control.

The first process, called "jidoka" (automation with a human touch), emphasizes the importance of quality during manufacturing. Under the system, manufacturing equipment is responsible for detecting product quality issues and immediately stops when problems arise. Defective parts can be attended to at the point of the problem, isolating production problems more quickly. The second principle focuses on waste elimination and promoting productivity by keeping only the necessary amount of inventory on hand, as anything more consumes excess capital, manpower, and space.

Source: Toyota.

By the 1980s, Japan had become a manufacturing powerhouse and was taking market share away from US competitors. In that time, Japan had become the largest automobile maker in the world (with a 30 percent share), dethroning the US from the top spot it held since 1904.[13] Further gains in electronics subsequently drove many US manufacturers out of business. For example, US television manufacturers went from 27 in 1955 to 1 by the 1980s.

Japan today continues to be a major manufacturing force, particularly within the electronics, auto, and machinery industries.

Rise of the Tigers

Another major development was the market entrance of the four Asian Tigers—Hong Kong, Singapore, Taiwan, and South Korea. These nations went through massive industrializations from the 1960s through the 1990s. The push proved "miraculous" as economic growth during this period averaged over 8 percent annually. Exports grew markedly as well—from 1965 through 1990, exports from South Korea and Taiwan increased by 90 and 30 times, respectively.[14]

How did they do it? Like Japan, the government played a crucial role in the development of the Asian Tigers. Through the promotion of education, savings, trade, and technology, these nations began flourishing and manufacturing output rose substantially.

The Promotion of Education   The Asian Tigers believed in the merits of education and were strong promoters of school for both females and males, which isn't common across industrializing nations. Further, the Tigers focused their educational expenditures on primary and secondary school rather than universities, which increased the number of students who could be educated. The four Tigers had established universal primary education by the mid-1960s, ten years earlier than other countries of similar income levels, and at least three-fourths of all students attended secondary schools by 1987.[15]

In Taiwan, for example, the percentage of 12- to 14-year-olds in school rose from 23 percent in the early 1950s, to 85 percent in the 1970s, and 100 percent in the early 1980s.[16] This educational focus was important, as it helped promote a meritocracy and productivity, leveling the playing field between the rich and poor, and it encouraged hard work and training. As a result, extra education and tutoring became common, provided both by tutors and mothers who had the educational background to provide academic assistance.

Promotion of Saving and Investment   Like Japan, East Asia has high savings rates, which provided the necessary capital for new investment. Both private investment and bank savings were encouraged as capital gains and interest earned on savings were largely untaxed, thereby increasing the financial benefit of saving, and inflation was kept largely in control compared to other low- and middle-income countries.

East Asia's government also encouraged private investment by providing tax breaks for favored industries (similar to Japan) and maintaining capital controls on money leaving the country.

Promotion of Trade   The Asian Tigers were large promoters of trade and exports in part because of the small size of their domestic economies and limited natural resources. To grow, these countries focused outward in search of new market opportunities and increased technical ability. Policies pointed at achieving this growth differed among countries but were generally focused on promoting exports, encouraging new investments, and restricting imports.

Governments promoted competitiveness by keeping wages down and maintaining favorable (and sometimes undervalued) exchange rates to keep manufacturing costs low. In Hong Kong, for example, the government constructed low-income housing, controlled food prices, and kept education and transportation at preferential rates. The impact of these subsidies, adding an estimated 50 to 70 percent to income, reduced the pressure to increase wages, which kept manufacturing costs low.[17]

One famous example occurred in South Korea. Monthly, the South Korean government would sit down with executives at major corporations to discuss export plans and their views of the market and to evaluate how well these companies were meeting their goals. These meetings not only kept exports as a focus, but they also provided large gains in the way of cheap credit and tariff protection for those companies able to successfully accomplish their goals. Unsuccessful companies faced potential penalties and in some cases were driven to bankruptcy. By the mid-1980s, government involvement in business was lessening, and the frequency of these meetings began to decrease.

Promotion of Foreign Investment and Technology   The East Asian governments were typically open to foreign investment. For example, most countries created SEZs for investment. The benefits of investing in these areas included favorable investment terms such as exemptions on duties and regulations, removal of tariffs on imported machines and raw materials, favorable tax rates, and land provisions. These policies encouraged foreign direct investment as foreign multinationals looked to take advantage of the relatively cheap and educated labor forces. This labor was primarily non-unionized in the conventional sense as Singapore, Taiwan, and Korea abolished trade-based unions during this time (company-based unions were encouraged, however).[18]

Though open to foreign investment, each Tiger nation individually had varying degrees of openness. For example, Korea required that local market investment come through joint ventures with local manufacturers. Like Japan, purchases of technology licenses from foreign markets were also common.

Conversely, Hong Kong has very few restrictions on money moving in and out of the country, almost no import barriers, and, with few exceptions, is open to most companies looking to establish a new manufacturing base. This is one reason Hong Kong ranks so highly on foreign direct investment performance metrics. Between 2005 and 2007, Hong Kong ranked highest in the world on the United Nations' Inward FDI Performance Index (at 8.652), which is the ratio of a country's share of global FDI inflows to its share of global GDP.[19]

The Changing Nature of Exports   Focus on exports has changed over the years as technology, competition, and opportunities have changed. The focus has shifted first from light manufacturing (textiles), to heavy manufacturing (automobiles, ships, steel), to now higher value-added goods such as electronics, semi-conductors, and computers in anticipation of a loss of competitive advantage in labor-intensive sectors.

A good example is Taiwan. By the 1960s, textile manufacturing began to get re-directed out of the country to lower wage countries like China. An appreciating currency and rising wages in the latter part of the 1980s also decreased Taiwan's competitiveness and led to money leaving the country in search of cheaper alternatives. To counter such issues, the Taiwanese government re-focused its investment efforts to "high-technology" goods that require significant research and development costs such as biotechnology, machinery, precision instruments, and electro-optics. In 1984, the government began providing tax incentives for manufacturers who utilize research and development toward improving and diversifying product lines.

China's Rise

From the time China opened its doors in 1979 through 2003, exports and imports grew at an average rate of 15 percent per year, compared to a 7 percent annual growth in world trade over the same period.[20] By 2007, China's total trade had risen to $2.2 trillion—up from $20.6 billion in 1978.[21]

So what drove this remarkable growth and the shift in manufacturing power? The liberalization of the economy and the country's general structure as an "assembler" of final goods are among the most important changes.

China Opens Its Doors   The man most often credited for changes in China was Deng Xiaoping, the Chinese head of government from 1978 through the early 1990s. Unlike popular thought at the time, Deng encouraged the use of a market economy and capitalist-like enterprise, later to be frequently called "market socialism."

One of Deng's first reforms was decentralizing the farming sector to allow farmers to cultivate and lease their own family plots. While the government still owned the land and required rent payments each month (often in agricultural goods), farmers were able to produce whatever goods they liked and could charge whatever they wanted.

This is much different than China's farming industry prior to 1978. Before decentralization, Chinese farmers were rewarded "work points" for their farm production, but they were given little incentive to expand production since these points were not based on output. The reform proved very successful, with food production and farming variety increasing quickly. Farmers were subsequently also allowed to start new side businesses and keep any profits they generated. And what initially started as roadside markets to sell crops had, within a few years, expanded into other industries such as light manufacturing, restaurants, and stores.[22]

The early success of farming reform spurred greater openness and ultimately the expansion into manufacturing. Deng opened China to all imports and began encouraging foreign investment. Like its

Asian peers, China established SEZs to attract foreign capital. While his reforms were controversial and support for them waned over the years, Deng remained committed to attracting foreign capital. "There are those who say we should not open our windows, because open windows let in flies and other insects," Deng said. "They want the windows to stay closed, so we all expire from lack of air. But we say, 'Open the windows, breathe the fresh air and at the same time fight the flies and insects.'"[23]

Deng's Persecution

Deng overcame great hurdles and persecution to gain office and institute his market reforms. Deng's ideologies were often criticized and fervent adversaries threatened his life and removed him from power on more than one occasion. Throughout his political career, Deng was dethroned three times, placed under house arrest, paraded in a dunce cap through Beijing, made to wait tables at a Communist Party school, and his son was thrown out of a four-story window.

Source: Steven Mufson, "Deng's Successor to Lead Memorial Rites Tuesday," *Washington Post* (February 21, 1997).

This capitalistic attitude and market openness ultimately drove significant increases in foreign capital, with multinationals taking advantage of the large and cheap labor force. Figure 2.4 charts foreign direct investment in China from 1980 through 2007. As the graph shows, investment significantly accelerated beginning in the late 1990s and continued its upward trajectory through 2007 when investment hit $83.5 billion (the fifth most of any country in the world).

This direct foreign investment created new jobs, brought new technology to the country, provided new training, and strengthened China's link to the global economy.

Trade liberalization reached a milestone in 2001, when China was admitted to the World Trade Organization. The result was a continued decrease in China's tariffs (falling from a weighted average

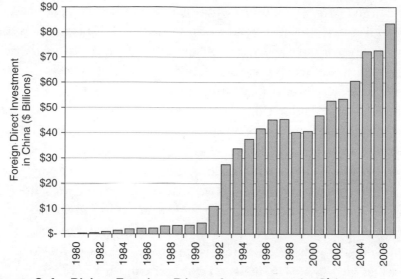

Figure 2.4   Rising Foreign Direct Investment In China
Source: United Nations.

of 40.6 percent in 1992 to 10 percent by 2005), and subsequently the removal of a number of import restrictions that were in place with the country's trading partners.

Change in China's Exports   Like Japan and the Asian Tigers, China's exports have changed as general openness, sophistication, and investment increased. Prior to the first phase of reforms, agriculture employed nearly 80 percent of the workforce, and China relied on its natural resources like oil, minerals, and agricultural goods in trade. But when reforms and investment took hold, the structure of exports began to shift away from primarily natural resources, and by 1986 exports of textiles and clothing exceeded that of crude oil. By the early 1990s, a significant portion of exports came from the production of low-sophistication light manufactured goods like clothing, footwear, textiles, and toys. Farming employment decreased to only one in two people by 1994—a reflection of increased manufacturing work and improved farm productivity and mechanization.

As time progressed, more sophisticated goods were manufactured on a greater scale. For example, machinery and transport exports (including electronics) increased in share from 17 percent in 1993 to 41 percent in 2003.[24] By 2004, China had an 11 percent share in world machinery exports, up from 2 percent in 1994.[25]

However, it's interesting to note the importance "process" trade has had on the country's exports. In process trade, China imports the necessary parts and components and is responsible for using the required inputs in the production of the final good. The final product is then shipped to the importer, who is responsible for selling the final product. Thanks in part to the growing technical abilities of its Asian peers, China has a local market to source components for use in production. Highly technical electronic components from Japan and Korea (as well as the US) are good examples of this.

As seen in Table 2.3, process trading accounted for 55 percent of all Chinese exports in 2007, up from 47 percent in 1992.[26] In very technical industries, the share can be much higher. Process trading in Chinese "advanced technology products" exports to the US accounts for 90 percent of all exports.[27] Process trading plays an important role in machinery exports as well, but is a much smaller share in relatively low-skilled manufacturing such as clothing.

The Chinese economy has grown markedly since market liberalization in the late 1970s, and with it has come a large change in the structure of exports and scale of production. In recent years, the share of more sophisticated exports has increased, which has been driven by increased sourcing of high-technology components from abroad.

Table 2.3   Process Trading in China

Exports	1992	1995	1997	1999	2001	2003	2005
Total Exports ($ Billion)	$84.9	$136.5	$160.3	$163.8	$211.2	$334.5	$525.5
Processing Exports ($ Billion)	$39.9	$67.9	$87.6	$92.2	$117.0	$184.6	$287.2
Processing Share	47%	50%	55%	56%	55%	55%	55%

Source: Amiti and Freund (2008).

THE STATE OF US MANUFACTURING

From a contribution standpoint, US manufacturing is no longer as important to the economy as it once was. Manufacturing employment has fallen, services have become an increasingly larger part of the economy, and the contribution manufacturing plays on US GDP growth has decreased since 1950.

Despite this, US manufacturing is far from dead and continues to play an important role in the country. While competition and outsourcing have increased, US manufacturing output continues to rise, productivity continues to advance, and manufacturing profits in 2007 reached their highest level in history.

The Decreased Importance of US Manufacturing

One of the most significant changes to the US since World War II has been the growth in service-related industries to the US economy as a whole. Figure 2.5 shows value added (sales minus gross input costs) as a percent of total US GDP from 1947 through 2007 for

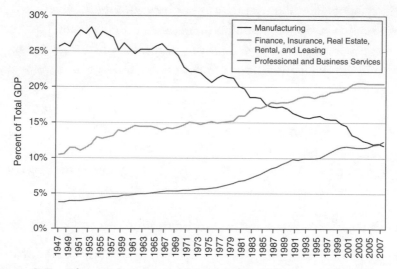

Figure 2.5   The Rising Importance of Services on the US Economy

Source: Bureau of Economic Analysis.

manufacturing, financial services, and professional and business services. Manufacturing peaked in 1953 at 28 percent of GDP and has progressively fallen since. Services, meanwhile, steadily advanced, growing from 48 percent of GDP in 1947 to 68 percent by 2007.

Of particular note is the fall in manufacturing of non-durable goods (goods meant to be consumed within three years, such as textiles and clothing), whose share of GDP decreased from 13 percent in 1947 to 5 percent in 2007 as production moved offshore to take advantage of cheaper labor markets.

High-skill service industries like financial and legal services have grown in importance with the expansion of their markets. These industries have historically been difficult to outsource as location, specialization, ease of communication, and advanced training are generally required. Service-related industries like education and financial services have also increased as consumer spending habits have changed and consumer wealth has increased. As we will later discover, service price inflation plays a role in this as well.

The shift to overseas manufacturing and increasing cost competitiveness from overseas suppliers have been met with technological advancements like robots and automation equipment, which removed the need for low-skill manufacturers as well. The result has been a decrease in manufacturing employee needs. Figure 2.6 charts manufacturing employment from 1950 through 2007, both in total numbers and as a percent of the total US workforce.

By the end of 2007, there were 3 percent less people working in manufacturing than in 1950, despite the size of the US workforce growing by 177 percent during that time. US manufacturing employment peaked in 1979 at over 20 million (20 percent of the total workforce) and has continued to fall since.

Manufacturing's Place in the US Economy

The decreasing importance of manufacturing should not be construed as an indication that manufacturing in the US is dead or unimportant. Quite the contrary. In fact, manufacturing increased faster and

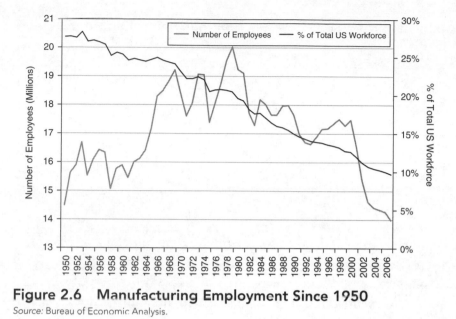

Figure 2.6   Manufacturing Employment Since 1950
Source: Bureau of Economic Analysis.

productivity improved greater than the overall economy. Take a look at Table 2.4, which shows the average growth in US manufacturing productivity (output per hour) and the non-farm economy between 1960 and 2007. As the table indicates, manufacturers have become more productive with their labor. This is largely a result of improved technology, advances in the automation of factories, and the successful incorporation of manufacturing processes like Six Sigma and lean manufacturing. The implementation of Six Sigma in recent years has paid enormous dividends for a number of manufacturers, who tout these programs as a means of eliminating troublesome production bottlenecks, reducing costs, streamlining operations, and improving product quality in the process. For example, Motorola estimated it saved $17 billion between 1986 and 2004 as a result of the program. (For more on Six Sigma, revisit Chapter 1.)

With improved production and increased efficiency, fewer employees are required to produce more output. This is one reason

Table 2.4   Average Growth in US Productivity (Output per Hour)

Period	Manufacturing	Non-Farm Business
1960–1969	2.6	2.7
1970–1979	2.6	1.7
1980–1989	3.0	1.6
1990–1995	3.4	1.5
1995–2000	4.4	2.1
2000–2007	3.7	2.1

Source: Bureau of Labor Statistics and William Strauss.[28]

that, while the number of people working in manufacturing has fallen, total manufacturing production has increased faster than the overall economy. From 1959 through 2007, manufacturing output increased by 410 percent, eclipsing the 373 percent inflation-adjusted growth of the US economy during that time.[29]

The link between productivity and total output is nowhere more striking than in the farming industry. Over time, technology, innovation, and changes in farm structure drove large productivity gains, which lessened the need for equipment, labor, and energy, even with output increasing. Figure 2.7 charts this phenomenon. The left y-axis charts total farm output, input, and productivity (difference between growth of agricultural output and the growth of all inputs) since 1977, while the right y-axis charts the number of farm employees annually.

The gains from productivity can be significant. As Figure 2.7 shows, even though farm employment dropped nearly 44 percent between 1977 and 2006, farm output actually increased by nearly 70 percent.

Increases in manufacturing productivity have helped manufacturers keep inflation pressures and cost increases contained, especially relative to service industries where prices have advanced markedly. A look at the cost of services relative to durable goods since 1959 reveals a growing spread between prices. Figure 2.8 graphs the PCE deflator, a measure of US inflation, for services and durable goods (goods meant to be used for more than three years) from 1959 through 2007. Durable goods data are used as a proxy for manufacturing

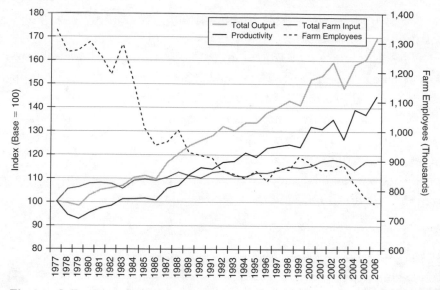

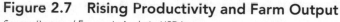

Figure 2.7   Rising Productivity and Farm Output

Source: Bureau of Economic Analysis, USDA.

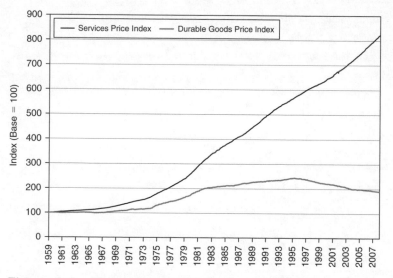

Figure 2.8   Rising Service Inflation, Falling Durable Goods Costs

Source: Thomson Datastream.

in this graph. While service prices continue to rise, durable goods inflation has actually *fallen* since 1995.

The disproportionate growth in service price inflation allowed services to take a greater share of the total US economy, even with output lagging behind that of manufacturing.

When analyzed in combination, one can see the US manufacturing industry is still an important and growing part of the economy. While its contribution to the total workforce and GDP growth may be shrinking, the fall is more reflective of improvements in technology and contained inflation than decreases in output.

Chapter Recap

The world's manufacturing landscape has changed significantly since the end of World War II, with globalization and new growth in Asia driving production to low-cost labor countries. These trends—coupled with rising productivity and technological improvements—decreased manufacturing's share of total US employment and its share of the economy.

- Increased foreign direct investment, increased trade, and cross-border mergers are evidence of globalization.
- Financial market and trade liberalization drove increases in global trade and investment.
- Asia's pro-growth policies—first in Japan, then later in the Four Asian Tigers (South Korea, Taiwan, Hong Kong, and Singapore) and China—drove significant export growth and shifted the world's manufacturing landscape.
- Increased overseas manufacturing competition, rising productivity gains, and the success of new service industries have lessened manufacturing's impact on total US economic growth and its share of total employment.

3

INDUSTRIALS SECTOR DRIVERS

Simply looking for the best stock is the most common investor mistake. That may sound counterintuitive, but it's true. Unless you've got a firm grasp on a sector's fundamental drivers and how they impact industries and individual firms, it's a near hopeless task to choose the right stocks. High-level sector drivers often have equal, if not greater, influence on a stock's performance than unique firm-specific fundamentals, so accurately identifying sector drivers is a must.

Every sector has unique drivers relative to the broader economy, and they're not static—they constantly change. Therefore, what's vital for Industrials in 2009 may not be exactly the same in 2010. Investing environments shift too quickly for any definitive "rules" for all time. This is especially true for a sector as diverse as Industrials, which operates in many different markets and maintains a variety of drivers.

However, there are certain factors that are relatively timeless and likely will always be important. From a macro perspective, corporate and government spending are the most important Industrials sector drivers, as corporations and governments are Industrials' primary customers. These two drivers should shape any analysis when making

Industrials-related investment decisions. We'll examine each in a bit more detail in this chapter.

CORPORATE SPENDING

What drives corporate spending? The most important factors include:

- Economic strength
- Corporate financial health
- Access to cheap capital

Other factors, like regulation and tax incentives, can also impact spending, but to a lesser degree. And this spending is not only for new big-ticket goods, like a new factory manufacturing system or a new mining machine. Often, this spending is on high-margin equipment service or replacement parts. These revenues can make up a significant portion of overall firm revenues.

Economic Strength

As covered in Chapter 1, Industrials are generally economically sensitive and cyclical. Industrials' customers, who typically operate in cyclical industries themselves, are more apt to purchase equipment when economic conditions are good, so product demand tends to fluctuate with economic conditions. Economic strength can also boost optimism about the future, encouraging new investment as well.

New investment by the construction, manufacturing, transportation, and commodity industries is most important to Industrials as these are the sector's major end markets. Health Care and Utilities equipment purchases are also important, but to a lesser degree.

Construction Spending Construction spending—whether residential or non-residential—historically has been sensitive to economic growth, as shown in Figure 3.1. The graph charts inflation-adjusted US GDP growth against construction spending in new residential and non-residential structures, which typically trend together.

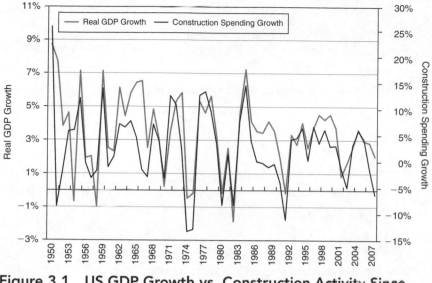

Figure 3.1   US GDP Growth vs. Construction Activity Since 1950

Source: Bureau of Economic Analysis.

However, be careful making judgments that both residential and non-residential construction will increase together. They don't necessarily move in the same direction or at the same magnitude. Historically, residential construction spending has been more volatile than both economic growth and non-residential construction activity.

Construction spending in turn is driven by a number of factors, including:

- **Available market supply.** Low available inventory of unsold homes encourages new construction activity.
- **Real estate prices.** High real estate prices encourage new construction because of expected profitability on new projects and increased property demand.
- **Vacancy rates.** Low vacancy rates may reflect strong property demand.
- **Consumer propensity to spend.** Economic factors like unemployment, consumer confidence, and income all contribute to consumer propensity to buy a new home.

- **Financing conditions and tax incentives.** Benign interest rates and government tax incentives lower purchasing costs and encourage investment. Project financing plays an important role as well.
- **Regional economic and population growth and demographics.** Real estate markets can differ dramatically by region depending on local market drivers like population and economic growth and demographic changes.
- **Input availability.** Land, materials, and construction worker availability affect project costs and the ability to complete a project.

Which industries tend to benefit when construction spending is strong? One of the greatest beneficiaries is the construction machinery industry, whose products support the construction of these facilities. Figure 3.2 highlights the link between inflation-adjusted US GDP growth and construction equipment spending from 1950 through

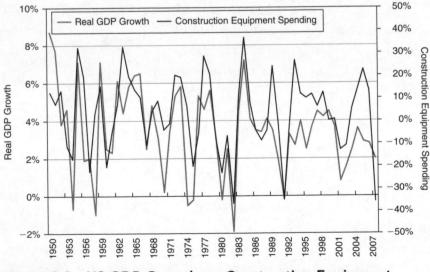

Figure 3.2   US GDP Growth vs. Construction Equipment Spending

Source: Bureau of Economic Analysis.

2007. While construction machinery demand varies by a wider margin than GDP growth, the link between the two factors is clear.

Outside of construction equipment, services such as general contracting and engineering, raw material transportation, and goods manufacturing (like electrical wiring, plumbing, security systems, air conditioners, and cabinets) all benefit from economic growth and increased construction spending. The major beneficiaries of increased construction spending include the following Industrials industries:

- **Aerospace and Defense.** Heating systems, air conditioners, elevators, and security systems.
- **Building Products.** Ceramics, glass, plastics, windows, faucets, cabinets, and other manufactured building materials (excluding lumber) for use in the construction industry.
- **Construction and Engineering.** Design, construction, and in some cases day-to-day operations of residential and non-residential facilities.
- **Commercial Services.** Waste management services.
- **Electrical Equipment.** Factory equipment, generators, turbines, solar panels, electrical cables, and wires.
- **Industrial Conglomerates.** Mixed exposure given the diversity of the industry, but includes durable goods manufacturing and products used in construction, such as energy-efficient heating, ventilation, and air conditioning (HVAC) equipment, lighting, and fire and security systems.
- **Machinery.** Machinery used in facility construction.
- **Transportation Industries.** Transportation of the goods (lumber, stone, aggregates, etc.) used in construction.

Manufacturing Economic growth can spur manufacturing activity, which in turn can increase profits. More profitable firms are better positioned and have greater incentive to either buy new or upgrade old equipment to expand production. Historically, high production

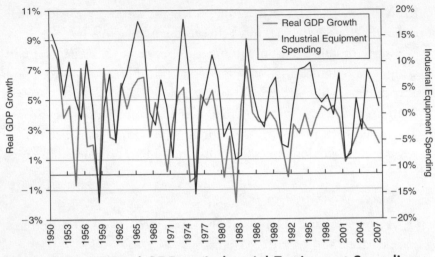

Figure 3.3   US Real GDP vs. Industrial Equipment Spending
Source: Bureau of Economic Analysis.

levels (usually around 80 percent of full capacity) have driven new factory investment as it indicates there is sufficient demand to expand output. Also, equipment tends to wear out with use, driving increased demand for replacement parts and service. Factory equipment for manufacturing plants (robots, automation systems, software, etc.) can be very expensive, making replacing an entire production system less likely as it is very costly compared to fixing problematic parts.

However, sometimes there is a need and incentive to replace entire manufacturing production systems. Technological advancements, changing product lines, and gains in productivity, product quality, costs, and manufacturing speed could justify new plant investment, for example.

Figure 3.3 shows inflation-adjusted US GDP growth relative to industrial equipment spending from 1950 through 2007. While industrial equipment spending is historically more volatile than GDP growth, the historical correlation has been strong.

Multinational firms' global expansion efforts, strong foreign economic growth, and increased production in lower cost regions have also driven manufacturing investment in recent years. US electrical equipment

Table 3.1   Emerson Electric and Rockwell Automation Foreign & Domestic Sales Growth from 2003 through 2008

Foreign Sales Growth	2003	2004	2005	2006	2007	2008	Average
Rockwell Automation	12%	13%	15%	9%	10%	23%	**14%**
Emerson Electric	10%	16%	11%	17%	22%	16%	**15%**

US Sales Growth	2003	2004	2005	2006	2007	2008	Average
Rockwell Automation	2%	4%	12%	13%	−22%	6%	**2%**
Emerson Electric	−5%	8%	10%	16%	3%	4%	**6%**

Source: Standard and Poor's.

manufacturers like Emerson Electric and Rockwell Automation reported strong foreign sales growth as a result. Table 3.1 shows annual foreign (non-US) and domestic sales growth for these two firms from 2003 through 2008. Foreign sales growth averaged over 14 percent for both firms during the period—much higher than the low to mid single-digit average growth witnessed in the US.

Outside of new equipment purchases, increased manufacturing activity also spurs demand for parts and components (also produced by many Industrials firms). Many of these products must be shipped to customers, which increases demand for freight transportation as well. The major beneficiaries of increased manufacturing spending include the following Industrials industries:

- **Electrical Equipment.** Factory equipment, robots, power generation equipment, and process management solutions.
- **Industrial Conglomerates.** Mixed exposure, given the diversity of the industry, but includes factory equipment and power generation products.
- **Machinery.** Heavy machinery and machine tools.

- **Trading Companies & Distributors.** Distribution of parts, components, and raw materials used in manufacturing.
- **Transportation Industries.** Freight transportation services via road, rail, ship, and plane.

Transportation Equipment   Many Industrials manufacture transportation equipment like ships, trucks, railcars, and airplanes, making the success of transportation industries vital to the sector as a whole. (Car manufacturing is the exception as autos are manufactured by Consumer Discretionary firms.) The manufacturing equipment used in making these goods, including car manufacturing, is often also produced by Industrials. For example, the auto industry has historically been the largest consumer of robotics, which are primarily produced by Electrical Equipment companies.

Transportation equipment demand is primarily driven by an overall growing economy and industry profitability. Increased marine freight rates, truck tonnage, rail volumes, and air travel demand are all driven by economic growth and help spur industry profitability and new investment. (We discuss where to find data on these metrics in Chapter 5.) Other factors such as replacement demand play a role as well.

Old and outdated equipment can be expensive to run, especially considering elevated energy costs and the opportunity and maintenance costs associated with equipment breaking down. For example, FedEx in 2008 allocated funds to purchase new Boeing 757s that are 40 percent more fuel efficient per unit than the aircrafts it was replacing. With jet fuel growing from 15 percent to 30 percent of airline operating costs from 2003 to 2007, the cost savings associated with new model upgrades can be significant.[1]

Regulation plays a role in transportation equipment demand as well, with firms purchasing new equipment to abide by new environmental standards. The US trucking industry provides one such recent example, detailed in the box on the next page.

Truck Emission Standards—Winners and Losers

In 2001, the EPA finalized its Highway Diesel Rule ("2007 Highway Rule"), which mandated a strict reduction in nitrogen oxide emissions and sulfur levels in diesel fuel. The mandates together were expected to reduce annual truck emissions by 90 percent, leading to the prevention of 8,300 premature deaths, 5,500 cases of chronic bronchitis, and 7,100 hospital visits. Beginning in 2007, all new trucks were required to have the new, environmentally friendly engines, which reduced particulate matter and nitrogen oxides and could handle the ultra-low sulfur diesel.

The adoption of these new engines caused cost and efficiency concerns within the trucking industry—the new trucks were expected to cost approximately $5,000 to $10,000 more than prior years, increase fuel costs between $0.04 to $0.05 per gallon, and result in a 2 percent reduction in fuel efficiency. The new engines were untested, creating reliability concerns as well.

To mitigate the impact, US truckers increased their orders in 2006 before the environmental standards took hold. This result was a great boon to North American truck producers, who recorded a banner years in 2006. Approximately 331,000 class 8 trucks were built in 2006, compared to the 230,000 normalized levels of years past.

Source: US Environmental Protection Agency; Securities Exchange Commission; Werner Enterprises.

Transportation equipment makers are concentrated in the Capital Goods industry group. The major industry beneficiaries include the following:

- **Aerospace & Defense.** Commercial aircrafts, engines, and business jets.
- **Industrial Conglomerates.** Aircraft engines and railcar manufacturing.
- **Machinery.** Ship construction, heavy truck manufacturing, and railcar manufacturing.

Aerospace & Defense firms, Electrical Equipment, Industrial Conglomerates, and Machinery all manufacture equipment used in transportation equipment production as well.

Commodities Demand A growing economy tends to increase demand (and prices) of commodities, including agricultural goods, metals, and oil and gas. Increased commodities prices tend to result in greater profitability for commodities producers, giving them more incentive to expand production and subsequently increase capital expenditures. The US farm industry provides a good example. Figure 3.4 shows profit growth for US farmers versus their machinery capital expenditures on a rolling two-year chart. Historically, you can see net farm income growth usually leads machinery capital expenditures.

Like other commodities producers, farmers tend to increase expenditures on machinery when they are financially able and incentivized to do so. For farmers, higher agricultural food prices encourage increased planting and the expansion of their crops, which often require new equipment. Higher profitability may also encourage farmers to seek tax breaks from new equipment purchases to lower their taxable income.

This relationship is seen in other commodities industries as well. Generally, higher profitability drives increased demand for new

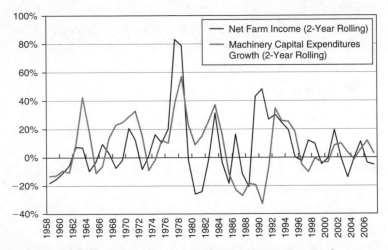

Figure 3.4   Net Farm Income vs. Machinery Capital Expenditures (2-Year Rolling)

Source: US Department of Agriculture.

equipment (tractors, mining equipment, oil ships, etc.), engineering services (consulting, technical services, project management, procurement, etc.), and new facility construction (new project design and construction). Increases in commodities demand also leads to greater transportation expenditures as these goods must be shipped around the world. As a major producer and provider of goods and services to commodities-related businesses, Industrials benefit significantly when commodities markets are strong. The following Industrials industries are most exposed to commodities:

- **Construction and Engineering.** Provides engineering, design, construction, and project management solutions for a number of commodities markets.
- **Industrial Conglomerates.** Provides varying exposure, typically similar to those in the Construction & Engineering and Machinery industries.
- **Machinery.** Produces machines and components used in commodities exploration and production.
- **Marine.** Provides long-distance bulk and energy transportation services such as the shipping of grains, metals, and oil and gas.
- **Road & Rail.** Provides freight transportation services for all types of commodities.
- **Trading Companies & Distributors.** Provides the necessary capital to take equity ownership positions in commodity projects around the world (this applies only to Japanese trading companies).

Freight Transportation Demand   Improved economic conditions spur increased consumer and corporate spending, which increases freight transportation demand as well. This includes shipment of raw materials, coal, consumer goods, food and grains, packages, and all exports and imports. And because transportation firms serve the freight needs for all sectors, transportation industries like Road & Rail and Air Freight & Logistics are often considered good barometers for the health of the entire economy.

The further liberalization and growth of trade will continue providing new market opportunities for transportation companies. As markets advance and trade grows, increased requirements will be placed on transportation firms serving the global economy. The long-term increases in trade should drive increases in port traffic, marine shipping requirements, and increased demand for intermodal services (where freight is transported by more than one form of transportation), among other things.

Corporate Balance Sheet Health

Corporate spending can't increase unless companies are financially able to do so. When available capital is scarce, firms are more inclined to focus expenditures on essential purchases (raw materials, production components, required service and maintenance, etc.) rather than on less necessary new equipment produced by Industrials firms. The operating life of many goods manufactured by Industrials is long, giving customers flexibility when they upgrade their infrastructure. As a result, firms may delay long-life, big-ticket purchases.

For these reasons, it's vital to understand the financial health of Industrials' customers and their end markets because that will dictate whether new purchases are likely.

Ease of Accessing Capital

Another driver vital to corporate spending is the ease of accessing capital, which generally manifests itself in benign interest rates. Generally speaking, the cheaper and easier it is to borrow, the more likely firms will take advantage to fund purchases. This spending can ultimately benefit Industrials. Note, falling or rising interest rates are less important than whether interest rates overall remain benign.

The ability to borrow cheaply has historically increased consumption as well. Benign interest rates may drive lower mortgage rates and spur construction activity. Lower borrowing costs can also increase demand for goods and, therefore, the need for transportation services.

GOVERNMENT SPENDING

Government spending is the second major driver for Industrials' growth as these firms are major beneficiaries of defense and infrastructure spending. Government healthcare spending is a benefit to certain industries, but the impact is more limited.

Defense Spending

The global defense market is huge—estimated at $1.3 trillion in 2007 and roughly 2 percent of global GDP.[2] Looking at just US defense spending in Table 3.2 gives a general sense of where demand comes from. Defense spending isn't just missiles and ammunition—employee compensation ($237.9 billion) and military services ($212.1 billion) accounted for nearly 70 percent of the $662.2 billion total.

Of the major defense programs not related to compensation or services, aircraft funding was the largest at $24.1 billion, followed by ships, vehicles, missiles, and then ammunition. Defense spending fluctuates with military demand, wartime needs, and the equipment upgrade cycle. Private firms bid on defense contracts authorized by the US Department of Defense. While these contracts range widely

Table 3.2   A Selective Look at US Defense Spending—2007

Name	2007 Value ($ Billion)
Employee compensation	$237.9
Military services*	$212.1
Aircraft	$24.1
Petroleum products	$12.2
Ships	$12.0
Vehicles	$8.8
Missiles	$8.7
Ammunition	$4.1

*Military services includes research and development, travel and transportation expenses, and installation, weapons, and personnel support.

Source: Bureau of Economic Analysis.

in size and services required, the largest contracts can drive significant increases in outstanding orders (known as backlog) and profits.

In recent years, spending has shifted from large, big-ticket items required in the Cold War to new, advanced technologies like satellites, communication equipment, and other systems designed to track down weapons of mass destruction and terrorists. Fighting terrorism, securing national borders, and deterring future wars all remain a focus for the Department of Defense.

A Contract for the Ages

In October 2001, Lockheed Martin beat out Boeing in the highly coveted joint strike fighter contract. The contract, worth potentially $200 billion, is the largest military contract in history. The planes, costing upwards of $50 million each, max out at nearly 1,200 miles per hour and can weigh up to 60,000 pounds when fully loaded.

Source: GlobalSecurity.com F-35 Specs; CNN, "Lockheed Martin Wins Joint Strike Fighter Contract," (October 26th, 2001).

While defense spending is an important driver for defense contractors, it should be noted that elevated defense spending doesn't always lead to industry outperformance. Note Table 3.3, which shows annual inflation-adjusted total defense and intermediate good defense spending growth against the American Stock Exchange Defense index and the S&P 500.

Table 3.3 shows there are years when defense firms outperformed, even with defense spending falling, and years when defense firms underperformed when defense spending growth was high. This is easily explained—the market discounts expectations for defense spending prior to the money being spent. Since 1997, defense firms have outperformed when the overall market was down and economic expectations were weak because defense spending is transparent and provides greater market assurance over operating conditions than other sectors where future demand is unknown.

Table 3.3   Total Defense Spending vs. Defense Industry Outperformance

Date	Total Defense Spending	Intermediate Good	Amex Defense	Industry Outperformance	S&P 500
12/31/1997	–3%	1%	30%	–1%	31%
12/31/1998	–2%	–3%	–1%	–27%	27%
12/31/1999	2%	7%	8%	–11%	20%
12/31/2000	–1%	–1%	37%	47%	–10%
12/31/2001	4%	10%	75%	88%	–13%
12/31/2002	7%	14%	1%	25%	–23%
12/31/2003	9%	17%	25%	–2%	26%
12/31/2004	6%	9%	32%	23%	9%
12/31/2005	2%	1%	10%	7%	3%
12/31/2006	2%	3%	25%	11%	14%
12/31/2007	3%	5%	41%	38%	4%
12/31/2008	7%	8%	–25%	13%	–38%

*Intermediate good purchases include military durable goods, nondurable goods, and military services like weapons and research and development.

Source: Global Financial Data; Bureau of Economic Analysis.

The Aerospace & Defense industry has the greatest exposure to government defense spending, but Construction & Engineering, Machinery, and Industrial Conglomerates provide military goods and services as well, including engines for military planes, research and development, training, engineering and technology services, and military base operations.

Infrastructure Spending

Infrastructure spending—spending on large-scale public services, systems, and facilities—is another major driver for the Industrials sector. The infrastructure market is large—over $400 billion in 2004 in the US—and spans a wide array of industrics. Table 3.4 shows US public (including local, state, and federal) and private infrastructure spending.

Table 3.4   Capital Spending on Infrastructure in 2004 by Category

Category	Public Spending ($ Billions)	Private Spending (% Billions)	Total
Schools	$75.9	$23.8	$99.7
Energy	$9.4	$69.0	$78.4
Telecommunications	$3.9	$68.6	$72.5
Highways	$66.7	$0.0	$66.7
Drinking Water and Wastewater	$28.0	$0.0	$28.0
Mass Transit	$15.5	$0.0	$15.5
Aviation	$12.4	$2.0	$14.4
Water and Other Natural Resources	$11.3	$0.0	$11.3
Freight Railroads	$0.0	$6.4	$6.4
Pollution Control and Waste Disposal	$2.6	$3.6	$6.2
Prisons	$2.9	$0.0	$2.9
Water Transportation	$2.4	$0.1	$2.5
Postal Facilities	$0.9	$0.0	$0.9
Passenger Railroads	$0.7	$0.0	$0.7
Total	**$232.6**	**$173.5**	**$406.1**

Source: US Congressional Budget Office.

Industrials aiding in construction services, such as Machinery, Construction & Engineering, Industrial Conglomerates, and Electrical Equipment, are the largest beneficiaries of infrastructure spending. These industries help with the design, construction, and electrification of these facilities.

Included in infrastructure spending is money allocated for alternative energy power (wind and solar) and energy-efficient products like lights and HVAC equipment. These industries generally all benefit from recent government "green" mandates and alternative energy funding. (Chapter 6 goes into great detail about the infrastructure market and the related investment opportunities for Industrials.)

Chapter Recap

Like any sector, Industrials has constantly changing drivers of varying importance. What's important in 2009 won't necessarily be a significant driver in 2010. But what will remain the same are the end markets the sector serves. To understand what's driving the Industrials sector, you must understand the health of its major end markets, including the construction, manufacturing, commodity, infrastructure, and defense markets.

- The Industrials sector is driven primarily by corporate and government spending.
- Economic growth drives construction spending, manufacturing, freight transportation, and commodity demand.
- Healthy balance sheets and cheap access to capital are important elements of corporate spending.
- A significant portion of defense spending goes to employment and military services. The remaining portion tends to fluctuate depending on military demand, new program initiatives, and the equipment upgrade cycle.
- The Construction & Engineering, Industrial Conglomerates, Machinery, and Electrical Equipment industries are most leveraged to private and public infrastructure spending.

II

NEXT STEPS:
INDUSTRIALS DETAILS

4

INDUSTRIALS SECTOR BREAKDOWN

Now you've got the basics of how the Industrials sector works, an understanding of its history, and its high-level drivers. But a high-level understanding is just the beginning. Just like our overall economy, the sector is made of many distinct parts—some relatively similar to others and some quite unique. To better understand the whole, you must understand the parts.

Chapter 1 covered the basic types of Industrials stocks: Capital Goods, Transportation, and Commercial Services and Supplies. But within those classifications, there are numerous types of firms with very different product lines, end markets, and drivers. While an understanding of every company isn't necessary, a firm grasp on the major industries is vital before making any sector-related portfolio decisions. This chapter explores the sector's industries and how an investor can begin forming opinions on each.

GLOBAL INDUSTRY CLASSIFICATION STANDARD (GICS)

Before beginning, some definitions: The Global Industry Classification Standard (GICS) is a widely accepted framework for classifying companies into groups based on similarities. The GICS structure consists of 10 sectors, 24 industry groups, 68 industries, and 154 sub-industries. This structure offers four levels of hierarchy, ranging from the most general sector to the most specialized sub-industry:

- Sector
- Industry group
- Industry
- Sub-industry

Let's start by breaking down the Industrials sector into its different components. According to GICS, the Industrials sector consists of 3 industry groups (Capital Goods, Transportation, and Commercial & Professional Services), 14 industries, and 24 sub-industries. Following are the industry groups and the corresponding industries and sub-industries for the sector.

Industry Group: Capital Goods
   Industries and Sub-industries:
- Aerospace & Defense
- Building Products
- Construction & Engineering
- Electrical Equipment
  - Heavy Electrical Equipment
  - Electrical Components & Equipment
- Industrial Conglomerates
- Machinery
  - Construction & Farm Machinery & Heavy Trucks
  - Industrial Machinery
- Trading Companies & Distributors

Industry Group: Transportation
   Industries and Sub-industries:
- Air Freight & Logistics
- Airlines

- Marine
- Road & Rail
  - Railroads
  - Trucking
- Transportation Infrastructure
  - Airport Services
  - Highways & Railtracks
  - Marine Ports & Services

Industry Group: Commercial & Professional Services

Industries and Sub-industries:

- Commercial Services & Supplies
  - Commercial Printing
  - Environmental & Facilities Services
  - Office Services & Supplies
  - Diversified Support Services
  - Security & Alarm Services
- Professional Services
  - Human Resource & Employment Services
  - Research & Consulting Services

GLOBAL INDUSTRIALS BENCHMARKS

What's a benchmark? What does it do, and why is it necessary? A benchmark is your guide for building a stock portfolio. You can use any well-constructed index as a benchmark—examples are in Table 4.1. By studying a benchmark's makeup, investors can assign expected risk and return to make underweight and overweight decisions for each industry. This is just as true for a sector as it is for the broader stock market, and there are many potential Industrials sector benchmarks to choose from. (Benchmarks will be further explored with the top-down method in Chapter 7.)

Benchmarks Differences

What does the Industrials investment universe look like? It depends on the benchmark, so choose carefully. The US Industrials sector

Table 4.1 Benchmark Differences

Sector	MSCI All Country World (Total World)	MSCI World (Developed World)	MSCI EAFE (Developed World Ex-US)	S&P 500 (Large Cap US)	Russell 2000 (Small Cap US)	MSCI Emerging Markets (Emerging Markets)
Consumer Discretionary	8.5%	8.9%	9.6%	8.4%	11.0%	4.8%
Consumer Staples	10.6%	11.1%	10.3%	12.9%	3.9%	5.8%
Energy	11.9%	11.6%	8.5%	13.3%	4.4%	14.9%
Financials	19.0%	18.6%	22.6%	13.3%	23.4%	22.8%
Health Care	11.0%	11.9%	9.8%	14.8%	15.3%	2.9%
Industrials	10.6%	10.9%	11.5%	11.1%	16.9%	7.7%
Information Technology	10.3%	10.2%	5.1%	15.3%	15.8%	10.8%
Materials	6.5%	5.8%	7.8%	2.9%	3.7%	12.8%
Telecom	6.0%	5.3%	7.0%	3.8%	1.2%	13.6%
Utilities	5.6%	5.7%	7.7%	4.2%	4.4%	4.0%
Total	100.0%	100.0%	100.0%	100.0%	100.0%	100.0%

Source: Thomson Datastream; MSCI, Inc.[1] as of 12/31/08.

looks very different from that of Europe, Japan, and emerging markets (EM). Table 4.1 shows major domestic and international benchmark indexes and the percentage weight of each sector.

Sector weights show each sector's size in the overall index performance. While Industrials is the second largest weight in the Russell 2000, it's the sixth largest weight in the MSCI EM. Why do Industrials have a larger weight in developed markets? Emerging market Industrials have not yet established the same size or scale of operations as their developed market peers and participate in fewer markets globally, resulting in a smaller index weight. The relatively smaller size of the service and defense markets in emerging markets versus the US also helps account for the difference between the Industrials sector weights in the Russell 2000 and MSCI EM. Commercial Services & Supplies accounted for 26.5 percent of the Industrials weight within the Russell 2000 as of December 31, 2008, but only 0.8 percent in the MSCI EM.

Wide sector weight deviations can also occur from country to country, as shown in Table 4.2, which includes selected countries from the MSCI All Country World Index. The US nearly triples the next largest country weight and is 12 times bigger than the largest emerging market weight of 2.3 percent for Korea.

Not only can sector weights vary, but so can industry weights— sometimes greatly, depending on the chosen benchmark. Table 4.3 shows the weight of each Industrials industry group and industry within each benchmark.

Understanding these weights allows you to make better portfolio weighting decisions, and it emphasizes the most important components to focus on. For Industrials, Capital Goods and Transportation make up the majority of the weight in most benchmarks, and therefore are the focus of much of this book.

Capital Goods' industries make up the bulk of the weight in most global benchmarks—the industries' firms are simply massive. Relative to other Industrials industries, these industries' firms generally have greater geographic diversity, operate on a bigger scale, have larger market caps, and therefore can generate more profits.

Table 4.2   Industrials Weights by Country

Country	Industrials Sector Weight
US	45.5%
Japan	17.7%
Germany	5.0%
UK	4.0%
France	5.2%
Korea	2.3%
Sweden	2.2%
Switzerland	2.7%
China	1.5%
Netherlands	1.5%
Canada	1.9%
Spain	1.3%
Australia	1.3%
Denmark	1.2%
Hong Kong	0.9%

Source: Thomson Datastream; MSCI, Inc.[2] as of 12/31/08.

A Concentrated Group

Another characteristic of the Industrials sector is the industries' weights are concentrated in relatively few, very large players. Table 4.4 shows the percentage weight of the 10 largest firms in each industry (using the MSCI ACWI). With concentrations ranging from 45 percent to nearly 100 percent of the industry, the largest firms truly dominate.

Often, highly concentrated industries have recognizable bellwethers considered representative of the industry as a whole. UPS and FedEx (Air Freight & Logistics), Lockheed Martin and Boeing (Aerospace & Defense), and General Electric and Siemens (Industrial Conglomerates) are good examples. While one should perform stock analysis prior to any company purchase, these bellwethers can provide some idea on how the industry is performing.

Table 4.3 Industrials Industry Groups and Industry Weights

Industry Group	Industry	MSCI ACWI	MSCI World	MSCI EAFE	S&P 500	Russell 2000	MSCI Emerging Markets
Capital Goods		71.9%	71.5%	69.4%	73.5%	59.7%	78.5%
	Industrial Conglomerates	19.5%	19.1%	13.8%	25.7%	1.8%	26.1%
	Machinery	15.6%	15.8%	16.4%	14.9%	18.9%	12.3%
	Aerospace & Defense	14.2%	15.1%	6.1%	25.3%	12.6%	2.3%
	Electrical Equipment	8.9%	8.9%	12.2%	4.3%	12.4%	8.1%
	Construction & Engineering	6.8%	5.6%	8.2%	1.6%	6.1%	23.6%
	Trading Companies & Distributors	4.5%	4.5%	7.9%	1.1%	4.0%	4.1%
	Building Products	2.5%	2.5%	4.7%	0.5%	3.8%	1.9%
Transportation		21.3%	21.3%	23.3%	20.2%	13.9%	20.7%
	Road & Rail	10.4%	11.0%	10.6%	8.9%	5.0%	2.1%
	Air Freight & Logistics	5.2%	5.6%	3.2%	10.5%	2.0%	0.0%
	Transportation Infrastructure	2.2%	1.8%	3.7%	0.0%	0.0%	7.4%
	Marine	2.0%	1.6%	3.3%	0.0%	1.0%	7.5%
	Airlines	1.4%	1.3%	2.4%	0.7%	5.9%	3.7%
Commercial Services & Supplies		6.8%	7.3%	7.4%	6.4%	26.5%	0.8%
	Commercial Services & Supplies	4.6%	4.9%	4.4%	5.0%	16.8%	0.8%
	Professional Services	2.2%	2.3%	3.0%	1.4%	9.6%	0.0%
	Total	100.0%	100.0%	100.0%	100.0%	100.0%	100.0%

Source: Thomson Datastream; MSCI, Inc.[3] as of 12/31/08.

Table 4.4   Concentration of Industrials Industries

Industry	Concentration of 10 Largest Firms
Air Freight & Logistics	100%
Building Products	95%
Professional Services	93%
Trading Companies & Distributors	90%
Industrial Conglomerates	87%
Marine	87%
Aerospace & Defense	80%
Road & Rail	78%
Commercial Services & Supplies	78%
Airlines	77%
Electrical Equipment	76%
Transportation Infrastructure	67%
Construction & Engineering	53%
Machinery	45%

Source: Thomson Datastream; MSCI, Inc.[4] as of 12/31/08.

What makes Industrials so concentrated relative to other sectors?

- **Firm size.** Market values of the largest firms simply outweigh their global peers by far. General Electric, UPS, and Mitsui are all examples.
- **Barriers to entry.** Some industries, such as Airlines and Road & Rail, have high fixed startup costs, creating barriers to entry. Technical expertise, scale, and government relationships drive similar concentration within Aerospace & Defense.
- **Government involvement.** Governments in some instances may elect to keep firms nationalized and/or provide preferential treatment and lucrative contracts to certain firms. This involvement has limited the number of industry players and made some of the larger firms with these contracts bigger. Aerospace & Defense, Air Freight & Logistics, Road & Rail, Transportation Infrastructure, and Trading Companies are examples.

CAPITAL GOODS INDUSTRY GROUP

Now that you know the general breakdown, we can examine individual industries in greater detail, starting with the Capital Goods industry group, as it represents the sector's largest weight.

As a reminder, the Capital Goods industry group breaks down into the following industries and sub-industries:

- Aerospace & Defense
- Building Products
- Construction & Engineering
- Electrical Equipment
  - Heavy Electrical Equipment
  - Electrical Components & Equipment
- Industrial Conglomerates
- Machinery
  - Construction & Farm Machinery & Heavy Trucks
  - Industrial Machinery
- Trading Companies & Distributors

What are some common characteristics in this industry group? Capital Goods industries are in the business of producing goods— they're generally capital intensive, manufacturing focused, and construction driven.

Aerospace & Defense

The Aerospace & Defense universe has two main segments:

- **Defense firms.** Airplanes, ships, submarines, ammunition, satellites, surveillance and electronic systems, and space systems.
- **Aerospace firms.** Commercial airplanes, engines, and industrial goods.

Defense Firms   Defense-related firms largely manufacture military equipment. The largest defense firms tend to be located in the US because

Table 4.5   The Top 10 Defense Firms in 2007

Company	Country	2007 Defense Revenue ($ Millions)	% of Revenue from Defense
Lockheed Martin	US	$38,513	92%
Boeing	US	$32,080	48%
BAE Systems	UK	$29,800	95%
Northrop Grumman	US	$24,597	77%
General Dynamics	US	$21,520	79%
Raytheon	US	$19,800	93%
EADS	Netherlands	$12,239	21%
L-3 Communications	US	$11,240	81%
Finmeccanica	Italy	$10,602	54%
United Technologies	US	$8,761	16%

Source: Defense News.[5]

of the size of the US defense budget relative to its global peers. In fact, 8 of the 10 largest defense firms are US based, as shown in Table 4.5.

Defense firms derive revenue by successfully bidding for government defense contracts. These contracts can be established for many years and are often awarded to more than one firm, often leading to substantial outstanding orders (known as backlog) and a significant number of new pending projects. For example, as of December 31, 2007, Lockheed Martin had a total backlog of $76.7 billion (83 percent more than its 2007 revenue)[6] and Raytheon was involved in 15,000 contracts.[7]

With outstanding contracts in the thousands and backlogs in the billions, it's easy to see why cooperation is vital in the defense industry. Firms often sub-contract peers to perform certain parts of a project (the electrical controls or the engines in an airplane, for example). As a result, it's not uncommon for firms to compete for a contract while acting as part of a team in another.

Generally speaking, Defense firms' backlogs will often include *fixed-price, time-and-materials,* and *cost-reimbursable* projects. These project types can dramatically alter a firm's profitability and significantly increase the importance of operational success.

Big Defense Protecting Against the Offensive

Global military expenditures in 2007 came to an estimated $1.3 trillion—representing approximately 2 percent of global GDP. That figure is up 45 percent from 1998.

The US alone spent $547 billion, representing 45 percent of the global market. To put it in perspective, that's 43 times the amount of money that all the *Lord of the Rings, Pirates of the Caribbean, Spiderman,* and the *Harry Potter* movies made worldwide as of this writing, combined.

Source: Stockholm International Peace Research Institute; IMBD.com.

- **Fixed-price contracts** are previously established and not subject to change. Since these contract prices are generally higher than the other two, potential profitability can be great and higher margins are achievable. More negatively, project hiccups or cost overrides can be financially devastating since extra costs have to be absorbed by the firm.
- **Cost-reimbursable contracts** allow reimbursement for "allowable costs" (as defined by the contract) and pay a fixed fee/incentive/award based on project execution. These are generally lower risk, but typically have smaller profit margin potential than fixed-price contracts. The costs incurred under these contracts can also be challenged by the government, which could potentially lower profitability as well.
- **Time-and-materials contracts** reimburse firms for materials costs and certain expenses and pay a fixed hourly wage for labor. The benefit is primarily risk control, as these projects mitigate labor and escalating input cost risks. Drawbacks are fees paid for labor; materials prices, which are usually capped; and actual labor hours, which can vary significantly from the negotiated rates—all leading to additional costs that have to be absorbed by the company.

Aerospace companies Aerospace firms manufacture non-defense related commercial airplanes and other industrial goods. Similar to their defense peers, airplane manufacturers will typically sign multi-year, multi-plane contracts and may sub-contract certain tasks to other suppliers. For example, Rolls Royce and General Electric manufacture aircraft engines used in both Boeing and Airbus planes. Like Defense firms, backlogs can be quite extensive. (At the end of 2007, Boeing had a total backlog of $327 billion.[8])

The commercial aircraft market is extremely competitive. The market for larger aircrafts—100 seats and above—is run by a duopoly of Airbus and Boeing, while the smaller regional and business jet market is governed by a number of smaller industry players like Cessna, Raytheon, Bombardier, Embraer, and General Dynamics.

Market participants are expected to increase moving forward given favorable market fundamentals and high potential profitability. For example, both Russia and China are designing new planes. Improving economic conditions, rising income levels, increasing airline market liberalization, and strong replacement demand is expected to drive commercial aerospace demand moving forward.

Boeing expects airline passengers and cargo traffic will increase 4.0 percent and 5.8 percent annually, respectively, from 2007 through 2027, while the number of planes in service will increase 3.2 percent annually. This traffic increase requires an estimated $3.2 trillion in new planes, providing opportunity for new market players.[9] Table 4.6 shows where market demand is expected to be derived. As the table indicates, the Asia-Pacific region is expected to show the greatest growth.

Building Products

Building Products firms are involved in producing home improvement and construction goods, including ceramics, glass, plastics, windows, faucets, cabinets, and other manufactured building materials (excluding lumber). Competition is a major issue for this industry because of limited barriers to entry.

While sales channels can differ, these firms generally sell through their own distribution channels to builders and contractors, as well as through retailers and home improvement centers. US home improvement manufacturer Masco and building material manufacturer USG

Table 4.6   Airplane Demand by Region Through 2027

Region	Total Market Value ($ Billions)	Total Deliveries	% Increase in Fleet Size
Asia-Pacific	$1,190	9,160	197%
North America	$740	8,550	55%
Europe	$740	6,900	68%
Middle East	$260	1,580	101%
Latin America	$140	1,700	119%
Russia & Central Asia	$60	950	12%
Africa	$60	560	60%
World	$3,190	29,400	88%

Source: Boeing Current Market Outlook, 2008–2027.

Corporation for example received approximately 20 percent and 11 percent of their sales from Home Depot in 2007, respectively.[10]

Building product demand is driven primarily by residential and commercial construction and remodeling activity, with renovations being the stronger force. According to US floor and ceiling system manufacturer, Armstrong World Industries, renovation work represents approximately two-thirds of the North American residential market opportunity and three-fourths of the commercial market opportunity.[11]

Company Spotlight: Saint-Gobain

Saint-Gobain, the world's largest Building Products company, insulates one-fifth of all homes in the US and manufactures 30 billion bottles, flasks, and jars a year. The company, founded in 1665, also supplied the glass for the Louvre in Paris.

Source: Saint-Gobain.

Construction & Engineering

Construction & Engineering firms provide diverse services to support infrastructure and construction activity globally. (Vinci SA even manages parking spaces in Europe.) While most firms tend to focus on transportation-related infrastructure (e.g., the construction of airports, railways, bridges, tunnels, and ports), a few also specialize in other services including power plant and oil and gas facility construction, government testing, and nuclear disarmament services. These projects are not quick to complete, sometimes taking years to finish, leading to significant backlogs and orders. The opportunities for these firms are large—an estimated $2.2 trillion is required to upgrade America's infrastructure and current estimates for emerging markets exceed that.[12] (Please see Chapter 6 for more on the infrastructure market opportunities.) Construction & Engineering firms operate similarly to the Aerospace & Defense industry. Firms generally bid on these government and private industry contracts and are awarded projects based on their technical expertise, prior track record, and bid competitiveness. The bids will factor in the terms of the deal, which is generally either a *cost-reimbursable* or *fixed-price* contract—a subtle difference in pay structure, but a huge difference in risk profiles (as previously noted).

Electrical Equipment

Electrical Equipment includes firms manufacturing electrical components and equipment (heating ventilation and air conditioning [HVAC] equipment, electric components, lighting fixtures), heavy equipment (power generation equipment, turbines, motors, circuit breakers, transformers, etc.), and automation equipment (robots, factory equipment, drive systems, software, and various other electronics used in automation). The firms generally serve utilities (electric, gas, and water) as well as manufacturing-related industries where factory automation equipment is used.

Alternative energy companies also play a major role in the industry, with a number of solar panel and wind companies often classified as Electrical Equipment companies.

Demand for these firms' products is primarily driven by global industrial production and capacity utilization levels, corporate capital expenditures, and manufacturing capacity investments (upgrades, expansions, new facilities, etc.).

Company Spotlight: Vestas Wind Systems

Vestas Wind Systems, the world's largest wind turbine company, has installed more than 35,000 wind turbines globally. Its turbines generate 60 million megawatt hours (mwh) of energy per year—enough electricity to supply millions of households.

Source: Vestas Wind Systems.

Industrial Conglomerates

Industrial Conglomerates have tremendous diversity in business lines and end markets. These firms tend to be holding companies, and the parent company has operational control and is the ultimate beneficiary of each segment's profits. Industrial Conglomerates can be seen as playing the role of a portfolio manager, buying and selling businesses out of their portfolio as desired. For example, well-known US conglomerate General Electric (GE) announced the purchase of 422 companies and assets between 2000 and 2008.[13]

Conglomerates are generally considered decent economic barometers because of their broad market exposure and participation in diverse industries. Example: GE sells, among other things, aircraft engines, water filtration systems, wind turbines, and medical equipment and owns a television network. While the industry is dominated by two of the world's largest firms, GE and Siemens, there are smaller firms with similar operating structures, diverse end markets, and drivers.

Machinery

The Machinery industry is split into two distinct parts—heavy machinery and industrial machinery.

- **Construction & Farm Machinery & Heavy Trucks.** Heavy-duty trucks and earth-moving equipment used in construction and infrastructure projects.
- **Industrial Machinery.** Industrial machinery and components for use in factories and equipment.

Construction & Farm Machinery & Heavy Trucks   Construction & Farm Machinery & Heavy Trucks firms produce heavy-duty commercial trucks, construction and farm machinery (often very large, see the box below), and non-defense related ships. Major equipment manufacturers have historically been from the US (Caterpillar, Deere, and Paccar), Japan (Komatsu, Mitsubishi Heavy, and Kubota), and Europe (Volvo, Scania, and CNH Global), where demand has been strongest. More recently, South Korean companies have become competitive with large-scale ship demand being strong (Hyundai Heavy, Samsung Heavy, and Daewoo Shipbuilding are the world's largest shipbuilders) and after Doosan Infracore purchased the Bobcat machinery unit from US manufacturer Ingersoll Rand in 2007. The market for construction, agricultural, mining, and oilfield machinery is large, with US machinery sales reaching nearly $61 billion in 2007.[14]

The Liebherr T 282 B

The $3.5 million Liebherr T 282 B is the world's largest truck with a maximum operating weight of 652 very huge tons. The 10.4 ton, 3,650 hp engine holds 1,250 gallons of fuel and consumes 35 to 45 gallons of diesel per hour.

Demand has historically been strongest in developed nations—the US, Western Europe, and Japan—where technology and machinery innovation is important. In recent years, emerging markets have become a major growth driver as well.

The major industry players all have extensive global distribution channels to sell their equipment—Caterpillar's 181 dealers sell to 182 countries[15]—but in recent years, they have also begun selling a substantial amount of equipment to rental companies, who purchase the equipment to be rented out for short- and long-term periods. These companies now purchase a significant amount of new equipment and can have a large impact on total industry sales and prices. The rental industry has large diversified machine fleets and flexible rental periods, which gave customers more flexibility and cost control when deciding between purchasing new or renting old equipment.

Monster Caterpillars

In 1905, photographer Charles Clements caught a glimpse of the Holt No. 77, one of the two tractor manufacturers that started Caterpillar. In awe of its design and movements, Clements exclaimed, "If that don't look like a monster caterpillar." The name stuck, and by 1910, "Caterpillar" had become a registered trademark of Holt Manufacturing Company. The company later merged with CL Best Tractor Co. in 1925 and became Caterpillar Tractor Co. In 1986, the company's name was changed to Caterpillar Inc.

Source: The History of Caterpillar, Caterpillar website; Eric Orlemann, *The Caterpillar Century*, (Motorbooks: 2007).

While the rental market had been established for a while in the UK and Japan, the industry in the US really began to take hold in the 1990s when local and regional rental companies merged to become national and large regional companies. However, the industry is still highly fragmented, with 6,500 market participants, and the 10 largest players in the US accounting for less than 25 percent of industry revenue, according to United Rentals, the largest US machinery rental company. Figure 4.1 charts the sales growth of the US rental industry since 1990. Since that time, revenues grew an average of over 10 percent a year.[16]

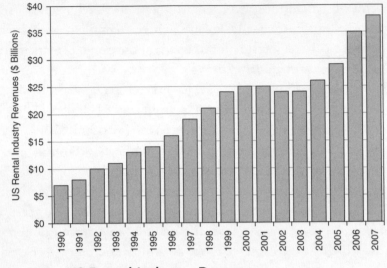

Figure 4.1   US Rental Industry Revenues
Source: United Rentals.

Industrial Machinery   Industrial Machinery firms make machine tools and machine presses, but also tend to focus on non-stand-alone items like flow control systems, valves, pumps, and other factory and machinery components. The industry is diversified, both geographically and in end markets (Parker-Hannifin boasts that in 2007, its 427,000 clients all mostly came from the manufacturing, transportation, and processing industries[17]), making them difficult to analyze in aggregate. In general, however, these firms sell their products to other businesses and will be driven by the strength of their customers' end markets, company replacement cycles, corporate reinvestment and capital expenditures, high industrial production and capacity utilization.

Trading Company & Distributors

Trading Company & Distributors vary greatly operationally and strategically, depending on the continent. In general, US firms are distributors (though some are also producers) of general manufacturing goods and construction supplies. Product offerings are typically very large (US distributor Fastenal stocks approximately 825,000 items, including over 225 different nails[18]) and diverse (everything from janitorial and safety goods to machine tools and paints). These firms use outside suppliers for a portion of their products, but also produce their own labels as well.

Conversely, Japanese trading companies part of the Keiretsu system are among the most diversified companies in the world due to their wide array of investments, joint ventures, and services—these include raw material procurement, financing, and commodity trading. For more on Japanese trading companies, revisit Chapter 2.

These Asian trading companies are structured similarly to Industrial Conglomerates—they act as holding companies and the ultimate beneficiary of each business lines' profitability. The investments can be quite diverse, with purchases recently being centered on natural resource positions, but have historically also included grocery stores, retailers, and real estate.

TRANSPORTATION

The Transportation industry group is broken down into five industries, two of which have sub-industries:

- Air Freight & Logistics
- Airlines
- Marine
- Road & Rail
  - Railroads
  - Trucking
- Transportation Infrastructure
  - Airport Services
  - Highways & Railtracks
  - Marine Ports & Services

Transportation industries tend to specialize in shipping different types of goods. Railroads and Marine firms generally specialize in shipping heavy goods like commodities and containers over large distances. On the other extreme are Airlines and Air Freight & Logistics firms who specialize in shipping low-weight, high-value goods for which delivery time is very important. In between these transportation modes is Trucking, the largest percentage of the freight market by revenue, which typically delivers lighter items such as food, clothing, and various other manufactured goods.

Air Freight & Logistics

Air Freight & Logistics firms provide services relating to the transport of goods, logistics, and e-commerce. Cargo delivery, an estimated $24.5 billion industry in the US in 2007,[19] makes up the greatest portion of revenues for the industry's largest firms—FedEx and UPS.

Globalization has also spurred new demand for global supply chain services as firms outsource a greater portion of their supply chain. According to transportation and supply chain management provider Ryder Systems, the global supply chain logistics market is worth an estimated $317 billion and growing, as new technologies are needed to counter the increasingly complex and globally diversified supply chains.[20]

Company Spotlight: United Postal Service (UPS)

UPS, the world's largest Air Freight & Logistics firm, delivered an average of 15.75 million packages per day worldwide in 2007 (peaking at 22 million packages during the holidays). That equates to 3.97 billion packages delivered worldwide for the year.

And while package delivery keeps the company busy, UPS has ventured into other markets including laptop computer repair. In 2004, the firm signed an agreement with computer maker Toshiba to ship, service, and repair the company's laptops. The agreement provided a new opportunity for UPS and faster repair times for Toshiba and its clients. UPS provides similar repair services for US firms InFocus and Lexmark International.

Source: SEC UPS Form 10-K; UPS company website; Arik Hesseldahl, "Toshiba Will Have UPS Fix Its Laptops," *Forbes* (April 27, 2004).

Airlines

Airlines provide global passenger and cargo air transportation services. In recent years, the US market has been plagued by a number of challenges, including higher input costs, overcapacity concerns, low-cost carrier competition, and weakening demand.

There are three main types of US airlines today—the major airlines, the regional airlines, and the low-cost carriers:

- **Major airlines** offer scheduled flights to most major US cities and a number of smaller US and global cities through a hub-and-spoke network. Examples include Northwest, Delta, Continental, and United.
- **Regional airlines** typically operate smaller aircrafts and work lower volume routes, where travel demand is less and runway size is smaller, usually in conjunction with major airlines. Examples include ExpressJet, American Eagle, and Horizon.
- **Low-cost carriers** generally offer limited passenger services, allowing them to offer lower fares. Low-cost carriers typically focus on direct flights to major cities where demand is expected to be strongest. Examples include Southwest Airlines, JetBlue, and Frontier.

Strange But True Facts About the Airline Industry

- The airline industry is one of the most heavily taxed in the US—taxes and fees account for approximately 14 percent of the total fare charged.
- When adjusted for inflation, airline fares fell 51.9 percent between 1978 (when US airlines were deregulated) and 2007.
- Atlanta was the busiest US airport in 2007. Over 42 million passengers came through the airport, and 992,000 planes either took off or landed.
- In 2005, Northwest Airlines announced it was canceling its magazine subscriptions and pretzel handouts on its flights. The plans were expected to save the company $565,000 and $2,000,000 per year, respectively.

Source: SEC JetBlue form 10-K; 2008 ATA Economic Report; Joe Sharkey, "Air Fare Fracas," *New York Times* (June 7, 2005).

Marine

Marine firms provide goods and passenger shipping services globally. Shipping is generally broken down into two types of cargo—*wet bulk* and *dry bulk*—which differentiate the ship type used and the applicable spot market price.

Dry bulk shipping is the transportation of bulky raw materials like coal, iron ore, steel, and grains that react badly to water. Demand is generally driven by the strength of the global economy and demand for food and commodities. Industry profitability is driven by freight rates, which are most commonly linked to the Baltic Dry Freight Index. The index, a daily calculation of shipping rates from around the world, can be extremely volatile as noted in Figure 4.2. The graphs chart the index from 1990 through 2008.

Wet bulk shipping is the transportation of wet goods, primarily oil and derivatives like petrochemicals and refined petroleum products, for major oil companies, energy traders, and government agencies. The industry itself is very cyclical (much like demand for oil), and profitability can fluctuate greatly given changes in demand, operating costs, and tanker supply. Much like dry bulk carriers, shipping rates are priced both through long-term contracts and the spot market, depending on the company's strategy.

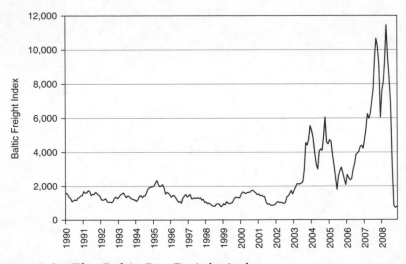

Figure 4.2   The Baltic Dry Freight Index
Source: Bloomberg Finance L.P.

Wet bulk transportation demand is determined by the markets the products serve. Bulk petrochemical volumes generally track economic growth, in part because demand comes from diverse industries like auto, consumer goods, housing, and textiles that use petrochemicals in production of their goods. Petrochemicals are also used in gasoline and are therefore sensitive to global gasoline consumption.

Gasoline consumption—by both autos and airlines—also drives shipping demand for refined petroleum products. Demand for the shipping of agricultural fertilizers is driven by the health of the farm economy and the production of farm commodities such as wheat, cotton, and corn.[21]

Road & Rail

Road & Rail firms compete for some business but generally operate in different markets and in different ways. Trucking firms tend to ship products shorter distances, and the goods themselves are lighter and more valuable. For example, US trucking firm Werner Enterprises received 46 percent of its 2007 revenues from the retail industry, 27 percent from the grocery industry, and 18 percent from manufacturing/industrial clients. Given the large size of the industry (an estimated $600 billion per year)[22] and the diverse needs of its clients, trucking firms have a diverse fleet, including trailers, dry vans, and flat beds. Because trucking firms have much more flexibility on their routes and generally go shorter distances, they tend to compete on service and efficiency.

The $54 billion[23] US Rail industry is much more focused on transporting bulky and longer haul shipments through its network of approximately 140,000 miles of tracks. In recent years, railroads have added fuel surcharges to their freight contracts, which mitigated the impact of higher fuel prices and helped boost industry profitability. Improved industry operations have had a significant impact as well.

While railroads ship a variety of goods, revenues are most concentrated in coal, chemicals, and farm products. Figure 4.3 breaks down revenue by commodity for the Class I railroads, the largest of the railroads in North America.

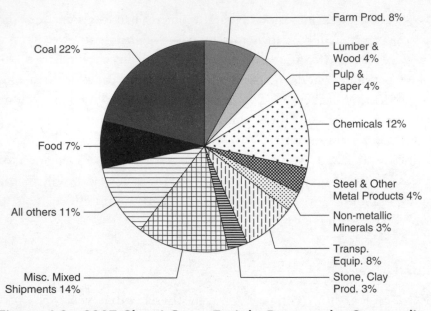

Figure 4.3   2007 Class I Gross Freight Revenue by Commodity
Source: American Association of Railroads.

The market is broken down into four main types of railroads:

- **Class I Railroads.** North American railroads with annual operating revenues in excess of $346.8 million in 2006. According to the American Association of Railroads, Class I railroads comprise only 1 percent of freight railroads, but make up 67 percent of the industry's mileage, 90 percent of its employees, and 93 percent of its freight revenue.
- **Regional Railroads.** North American railroads that have at least 350 miles of track and/or generate revenues between $40 million and the Class I threshold. A number of regional rail lines were created after the Class I divested ancillary rail lines. Like regional airlines, regional railroads generally maintain close relations with larger railroads and provide freight delivery service to smaller, less populated areas.
- **Local Linehaul.** North American railroads that operate less than 350 miles and less than $40 million per year in revenues.

Local linehaul railroads maintain similar characteristics as regional railroads, but operate on a smaller scale.

- **Switching & Terminal Carriers.** North American railroads provide transportation services within a specified area for one or more linehaul carriers.

Modern US Railroad History

US railroads have a rich history and played an important role in America's economic development. Westward expansion, population shifts, the accessibility of larger markets and raw materials, and increased industrial production were all made possible because of the railroads. Even the establishment of time zones was instigated by railroads.

Railroad's golden age ended by the middle of the twentieth century, railroads continue to play an important role in economic development and freight transportation. In recent years, these firms have gone through a "renaissance," driven by technological advancements, new market opportunities, and regulatory changes. Major changes to the US rail market since 1980 include:

- **1980.** The Staggers Rail Act deregulated the railroads, allowing firms to set their own pricing and streamlining asset sales to smaller rail lines. This spurred productivity gains and industry profitability and lowered inflation-adjusted shipping costs by 54 percent from 1980 through 2007.
- **1984.** The introduction of double-stacking containers on railroads, making railroads more competitive with trucks, spurring growth in intermodal transportation, and advancing globalization through cheap freight transportation. In 2003, intermodal revenues dethroned coal as the largest US rail revenue generator.
- **1994–1999.** Merger mania! Burlington Northern mergers with the Atchison, Topeka, and Santa Fe Railway in 1994; Union Pacific acquires Chicago and North Western (CNW) Railway in 1995 and Southern Pacific in 1996; Canadian National Railway purchases Illinois Central Railroad in 1999; and CSX and Norfolk Southern split Conrail's assets in 1999 after a multi-year dispute.
- **1998.** The North American Free Trade Agreement (NAFTA) establishes free North American trade, driving rail partnerships and new rail market opportunities in the process.
- **2004.** Railroads began to increase rail pricing and implement fuel surcharges. This was driven by many factors, including high energy prices, a rebound in economic

(Continued)

growth, limited rail capacity, rail contract renewals, increased value of shipped goods, and trucking market challenges. Railroad shipping prices increased on average by 7.7 percent between 2004 and 2008—much higher than the average 1.3 percent between 1996 and 2003.

Source: Bureau of Labor Statistics and the American Association of Railroads.

Transportation Infrastructure

The Transportation Infrastructure industry consists of firms that provide a wide array of infrastructure-related services, including the operation of ports, highways, and airports.

Pure play publicly traded infrastructure firms in the US are rare because infrastructure services are typically provided by private firms, government agencies, or alternative investment firms like private equity companies. As such, the global market for transportation infrastructure firms is much more concentrated in Europe and Asia. Of the 50 largest transportation infrastructure firms in the world, 42 of them are domiciled in one of these two markets.

The main markets are:

- **Motorway/Toll Roads.** Motorway and toll-road operators are responsible for the construction and maintenance of highways and toll roads and, in return, make money through toll-road fees. Much like a utility, rates are typically charged governed by the government.
- **Port Operations.** Port operators are responsible for the daily operations of ports. While some countries continue to view ports as strategic assets (e.g., DP World attempting to buy P&O operations in 2007), globally, the market is trending toward much more liberalization and privatization. In general, port operators receive revenues from the shipping companies accessing their ports, and in return pay a fee to the land owner for the use of the land (which today is usually the local government).

- **Parking Lots.** Parking lot operators design, build, and/or operate parking garages. The industry tends to be less regulated than other infrastructure-related industries, and as such, it experiences fewer barriers to entry and less government intervention. Business strategies within the industry can differ—some car park companies own the land on which they operate, while others simply provide the property and parking fee collection services.
- **Airport Operations.** Airport operators are responsible for airport servicing, including fueling and other fuel-related services, aircraft parking, hangar rental, and catering.

COMMERCIAL & PROFESSIONAL SERVICES

The last and smallest Industrials industry group is Commercial & Professional Services. These firms provide a wide array of business-related services including commercial printing, janitorial services, business consulting, and human resource management. The industry group is broken down into two industries—Commercial Services & Supplies and Professional Services.

Commercial Services & Supplies

Commercial Services & Supplies firms are engaged in a diverse range of services. These companies are primarily service-based organizations and operate on a smaller scale than Capital Goods and Transportation firms. And while the industry in aggregate is diversified, company operations tend to be focused on a niche part of the market. The industry typically works with other businesses, but some services like waste management and stationery carries over into consumer markets. Major services include the following:

- **Commercial printing and office supplies.** Commercial printing services, including books, magazines, checks, greeting cards, labels, paper, and stationery.
- **Environmental services.** Waste management services, including trash and medical waste collection and pest control.

- **Security and alarm services.** Security and protection services, including those required at correctional facilities, offices, and for secure money transportation.

Other industry services include storage and warehousing, commercial cleaning, uniform rentals, and auctioneering services.

Professional Services

Professional Services companies are primarily engaged in outsourced corporate advisory services, including the following:

- **Human resources.** Human resources services, employment services, outsourcing services, and corporate training. These firms recruit for a variety of industries and place both full-time and temporary workers.
- **Research and consulting services.** Corporate advisory services such as legal, business information, consulting services and testing, inspection, and certification services.

 Chapter Recap

The Industrials sector is comprised of a variety of industries that primarily serve other businesses and governments. The sector is made up of a diverse mix of manufacturers and service providers and generally serves multiple industries. The Capital Goods industry group, the largest weight in the sector, is composed primarily of manufacturers, including those producing electrical equipment, machinery, defense goods, and building products. Transportation services, the next largest weight in most diversified indexes, provide freight and passenger transportation services. Transportation via railroad, truck, ship, and air are included here. The remaining Industrials firms, classified as Commercial Services & Supplies, provide a diverse set of services including human resources, janitorial and security services, and commercial printing.

- The Aerospace & Defense industry is composed of defense contractors and commercial airplane manufacturers. The market is concentrated in the US, where product demand has historically been strongest.

- Building Products firms produce home improvement and construction goods such as cabinets, faucets, and ceramics. The industry is primarily exposed to the construction and remodeling markets.
- Construction & Engineering firms provide construction and engineering services globally. While these firms typically focus on transportation-related infrastructure, a selective few help build power plants and oil and gas facilities.
- Electrical Equipment manufacturers produce various electrical goods and components including power generation, factory automation, and HVAC equipment and components. Most wind and solar power firms are classified as Electrical Equipment manufacturers as well.
- Industrial Conglomerates serve multiple industries and produce a diverse set of goods. General Electric, the largest Industrials firm, manufactures wind turbines, aircraft engines, and medical equipment.
- Machinery firms construct farm machinery, commercial trucks, non-defense related ships, and industrial machinery. Drivers include industrial production, construction spending, and capital expenditure growth.
- Trading Company & Distributors in the US sell various industrial components, parts, and equipment and are primarily driven by the manufacturing industry. Japanese trading companies conversely have very diverse operations including raw material procurement, financing, and commodity trading.
- Air Freight & Logistics firms provide package delivery and supply chain management services.
- Airlines provide passenger and cargo air transportation services. In recent years, US firms have been plagued by a number of challenges, including higher input costs, overcapacity concerns, low-cost carrier competition, and weakening demand.
- Marine companies ship both bulk dry goods (like commodities and grains) and wet goods (like petroleum and oil). Industry profitability is driven by commodity demand and gasoline consumption.
- Road & Rail companies provide freight rail and truck transportation services. Trucking, the much larger of the two markets, primarily competes on service and tends to transport lighter, more valuable goods. Railroads tend to ship heavier bulk goods over longer distances.
- Transportation Infrastructure firms operate large transportation infrastructure including ports, toll roads, and airports. These firms typically service and at times construct these in exchange for service fees.

(Continued)

- Commercial Services & Supplies firms tend to operate on a much smaller scale than Capital Goods and Transportation companies. Services are diverse, including waste management, commercial printing, and janitorial services.
- Professional Services firms provide outsourced corporate advisory services such as consulting, human resource management, and legal support.

5

STAYING CURRENT: TRACKING SECTOR FUNDAMENTALS

It's not enough to simply understand a sector's structure and its drivers. To make forward-looking assessments, you must know how and where to monitor fundamentals impacting the sector most.

Industrials is a broad sector, so to help focus your analysis, this chapter highlights the most important and widely tracked metrics for monitoring the two most important drivers—corporate and government spending. A more comprehensive list detailing industry statistics and other good websites can be found in Appendix A. We'll also touch on the most important metrics to watch on an industry-specific level as well.

WHAT TO WATCH

Combing through government and corporate releases for nuggets of data helps analysts glean what the current sector landscape is and how that might impact future sector performance. It's not a crystal ball telling you what will definitely happen to a sector or an industry and how profitable it will be. And even if you had one, it wouldn't necessarily translate perfectly into a forecast for stock prices over any specific time frame. Why is that?

The economic statistics analysts pore over are a snapshot of what has already happened. Remember, the stock market is a discounter of all widely known information and moves based on future expectations. Keep that in mind when evaluating economic statistics, otherwise you risk placing ill-guided importance on something no longer meaningful.

Additionally, that snapshot is frequently imperfect, static, and doesn't provide the complete picture. Often, more qualitative analysis is required—reading company news stories, analyzing company earnings conference calls, and reviewing company investor presentations. These can be found through myriad news sources, firm websites, and the SEC.

However, economic statistics are helpful in evaluating the sector and shaping forward-looking expectations. Industry statistics can also be useful when comparing individual company results to its peer group. Recognizing a divergence between industry performance and company-specific results can provide insight on how a stock may perform relative to peers. Table 5.1 details some common and useful bullish and bearish Industrials statistics to follow. These and others are highlighted in the following pages.

CORPORATE AND GOVERNMENT SPENDING-RELATED METRICS

Because Industrials tend to be economically sensitive, a thorough evaluation requires broad analysis of economic health. At the highest level, monitoring gross domestic product (GDP) and other broad-based statistics provides an easy and comprehensive look at the total economy.

But for a more detailed understanding of the economy and important end markets, investors can monitor a variety of other industry and economic statistics. Manufacturing, construction, defense, infrastructure, and commodity-related industries are most important, as these are the sector's primary end markets.

Table 5.1 Bullish and Bearish Industrials Fundamentals

Bullish Drivers	Bearish Drivers
Increasing GDP	Decreasing GDP
Increasing industrial production	Decreasing industrial production
Increasing durable goods orders	Decreasing durable goods orders
Improving ISM manufacturing numbers	Decreasing ISM manufacturing numbers
Increasing construction spending	Decreasing construction spending
Increasing infrastructure spending	Decreasing infrastructure spending
Increasing defense spending	Decreasing defense spending
Increasing commodity prices	Decreasing commodity prices
Improving corporate financial health	Worsening corporate financial health
Cheap and easy access to capital	Difficulty accessing cheap capital
Increasing monthly sales orders	Decreasing monthly sales orders
Increasing rail volumes	Decreasing rail volumes
Increasing cargo volumes	Decreasing cargo volumes
Increasing truck tonnage	Decreasing truck tonnage

Measuring Economic Growth and End Markets

Outside of the commonly cited GDP figures, there are numerous ways to evaluate economic health, including statistics from various government entities and private organizations. These include:

- Business cycle indicators
- Industrial production
- Advance Report on Durable Goods Manufacturers' Shipments, Inventories and Orders
- The ISM Report on Business
- Business inventories
- Capacity utilization
- Construction spending
- Infrastructure spending
- Defense spending
- Commodities
- The Architecture Billings Index

GDP   *GDP* is the broadest economic indicator and one of the most cited, most forecasted, and most widely available economic statistics.

Detailed breakdowns of US GDP can be found on the US Bureau of Economic Analysis' website (www.bea.gov). Foreign and global GDP numbers are available through international data providers like the Organisation for Economic Cooperation and Development (OECD; www.oecd.org), the International Monetary Fund (IMF; www.imf.org), the World Bank (www.worldbank.org), and through individual country data offices (a full list of these websites can be found on www.oecd.org). A look at global economic performance is vital when analyzing the end markets of geographically diversified Industrials.

While GDP can be a useful metric, remember GDP growth is often volatile, can vary significantly from one quarter to the next, and reflects results from prior months. As such, investors should focus on the overall trend and expectations of future GDP growth rather than getting caught up with any single quarter.

Business Cycle Indicators   The Conference Board's *business cycle indicators* are good general economic growth barometers. The group produces three different indexes—the composite index of leading indicators, the composite index of coincident indicators, and the composite index of lagging indicators—which together explain the strength of the economy.

The leading index—an index made up of metrics expected in aggregate to reflect future economic conditions—tends to signal change before the coincident index, which in turn notes change before the lagging index. Both domestic and international data are calculated monthly and are available on the Conference Board's website (www. conference-board.org). The leading index aims to forecast future economic growth trends and is an important, though imperfect, indicator to watch for an economically sensitive sector like Industrials.

The indexes are unique in their use of metrics from multiple industries like average weekly manufacturing hours, industrial production, and stock prices. The full list of metrics used and index values can be found at the Conference Board's website (www. conference-board.org).

Industrial Production   *Industrial production* measures manufacturing output and is helpful in indentifying production trends for end markets. The data, released monthly by the US Federal Reserve (www. federalreserve.gov), is broken down in many ways by industry. While the top-line industrial production number is tracked and reported most, the Federal Reserve also reports production for individual components of the index, some of which are produced by Industrials firms, including agriculture, construction, and mining machinery, metalworking machinery, electrical equipment, and aerospace product and parts. Figure 5.1 shows industrial production of these industries (as defined by the North American Industry Classification System, or NAICS) from 1986 through 2008. The gray lines in 1990, 2001, and 2008 represent US recessions.

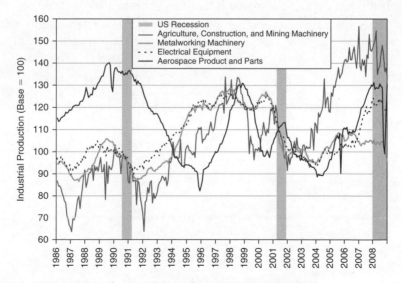

Figure 5.1   US Industrial Production Since 1986
Source: Federal Reserve.

As the graph shows, industrial production tends to slow during recessionary periods and re-accelerate in the subsequent recovery. The volatility of the data and their correlation to the economic cycle is a reflection of the sector's economic sensitivity. Table 5.2 further notes the average growth for each of the industries during growth and recession periods.

Note that Aerospace Products and Parts doesn't follow the pattern of other industries—on average, flat during recessions and growing less during expansions—because demand is dictated in large part by government military spending, which isn't economically sensitive. Historically, production for the Agriculture, Construction and Mining Machinery industry has fallen most during recessions in part because customers delay purchases until they are confident their respective markets have rebounded. For example, light machinery used in residential and nonresidential construction tends to lag housing starts by six to twelve months.[1]

Advance Report on Durable Goods Manufacturers' Shipments, Inventories, and Orders The monthly durable goods report is helpful when tracking demand for big-ticket items like those produced by Industrials firms. *Durable goods orders*—items produced to last longer than three years like cars, airplanes, and machines—is reported

Table 5.2   Industry** Growth During Recessions vs. Expansions

Industry	Average Fall During Recession*	Average Growth During Expansion
Agriculture, Construction and Mining Machinery	−9%	36%
Metalworking Machinery	−9%	13%
Electrical Equipment	−8%	15%
Aerospace Product and Parts	0%	7%

*The recession beginning in 2008 includes only data for 2008.
**As defined by the North American Industry Classification System, or NAICS.
Source: Federal Reserve.

monthly by the US Census Bureau (http://www.census.gov). The report is segmented into "new orders," "shipments," "unfilled orders," and "inventories" for a number of manufacturing-related industries like transportation equipment, machinery, and aircrafts—goods primarily produced by Industrials firms.

Shipments reflect what is currently being delivered, *unfilled orders* are orders that have yet to be produced, and *inventories* are the value of goods available for sale. The *new orders* section usually garners the most attention and is a helpful forecasting tool because it reflects future manufacturing production. The transportation industry is often omitted from the report because of the volatility involved in big-ticket orders like airplanes. As you review this report, remember, orders can be canceled.

ISM Report on Business®   The *Institute of Supply Management's* (http://www.ism.ws) manufacturing business survey is a good way to monitor manufacturing industry strength. Each month, the group surveys purchasing managers—those responsible for purchasing the inputs for production—from multiple industries to determine where manufacturing is trending. Participants are asked whether current conditions are "Better/Higher," the "Same," or "Worse/Lower" than the month prior for a number of metrics including new orders, manufacturing output, commodity prices, and backlog. (A full list of the metrics can be found on the company's website.) The survey results are aggregated and the findings are reported in the Manufacturing ISM Report on Business®. The group also compiles a non-manufacturing report, but the result is less meaningful for Industrials.

The data are presented in a seasonally adjusted "diffusion index," with any mark above 50 indicating growth and anything below 50 representing a contraction. This report is monitored closely by analysts as it's forward-looking and timely because it's released the first day of the month.

Business Inventories   The *business inventories* report by the US Census Bureau provides total sales data, inventories, and inventory-to-sales ratios for manufacturers, retailers, and merchant wholesalers. These metrics are important because they indicate current demand and how corporations are positioned for the future. Excess inventory may be reflective of weak product demand, possible future financial strain (inventory is usually financed with short-term loans), and future product discounting as firms try to eliminate excess inventory costs, free up warehouse space, and bring cash in the door.

However, some level of inventory is necessary to satisfy customer demand, which is why inventory-to-sales ratios are useful. The metric measures how long it will take to unload inventories at the current sales rate. Extreme values can prove problematic—too low a ratio and firms run the risk of selling out of goods, while too high a ratio may require production cutbacks. And while lean manufacturing techniques have helped mitigate the impact of excess inventories, firms are not always able to keep inventory at the optimal level.

Capacity Utilization   *Capacity utilization*, produced monthly by the Federal Reserve (www.federalreserve.gov) and reported in conjunction with industrial production, indicates the percentage of total production capacity currently being used. For practical reasons (including maintenance and repair), capacity utilization will almost never reach 100 percent. In fact, anything over 80 percent is generally considered strong—indicative of tight supplies relative to demand. Capacity utilization typically rises in high-demand periods as firms increase production to maximize sales, thereby encouraging new business investment.

High capacity utilization can have negative effects as well. High capacity utilization, particularly when it increases in a short period, increases the chances of component shortages, which could hinder future sales growth and may ultimately drive up product prices.

Construction Spending   As noted in Chapter 3, construction spending is driven by economic growth and is a major driver for many Industrials firms. *Residential* and *nonresidential construction data* are released monthly by the US Census Bureau (www.census.gov). The data are segmented a number of ways—by public and private spending, residential and nonresidential spending, and by market (office, power, educational, etc.). As one of the key Industrials' end markets, monitoring trends in construction spending is important.

Infrastructure Spending   While no perfect metric is available to monitor *infrastructure spending*, US government gross investment spending is commonly followed. The data can be found in the National Economic Account tables on the BEA website (www. bea.gov).

The "Government Consumption Expenditures and Gross Investment" table, released quarterly, breaks down expenditures by type (current expenditures and gross investment), government agency (federal, state, and local), use (national defense and non-defense), and gross investment classification (structures, equipment, and services).

The gross investment table is useful when analyzing fixed investment historically, but provides limited use in forecasting future spending initiatives. News analysis of proposed government spending plans is the best method of gauging future infrastructure and gross investment spending.

Defense Spending   National defense spending data are released quarterly alongside the GDP report and can be found under the "Government Consumption Expenditures and Gross Investment" section on the GDP tables. The BEA's "National Defense Consumption Expenditures and Gross Investment by Type" table breaks down defense spending by goods purchased. As noted in Chapter 3, not all defense spending goes to funding military equipment purchases.

An Overview of the Defense Budget Process

Defense spending is an important driver for many Industrials firms. But just how does the money get allocated to the defense budget?

- The White House and Pentagon prepare the budget request approximately 18 to 20 months before October 1st.

(Continued)

- The results are reviewed and edited by the Office of Management and Budget (OMB).
- The President approves the edits and submits to Congress.
- Congress and sub-committees review, make modifications, set funding levels, and ultimately approve both *budget authorizations* and *budget appropriations*.
- Budget authorizations cap the total amount that can be spent in aggregate on a particular project over its life.
- Budget appropriations grant the actual funding levels for a particular year for that program.
- It's very difficult to match up authorizations and appropriations in any given year as the appropriations bill could include authorizations approved many years before.
- Over its life, a defense budget is voted on 10 times in congressional committees and 12 times on the congressional floor.

Source: Mary T. Tyszkiewicz and Stephen Daggett, "A Defense Budget Primer," CRS Report for Congress (December 9, 1998).

The Department of Defense (DoD; http://www.defenselink.mil/) also produces defense-related news stories, including updates on defense budget spending and defense contract awards. If analyzing the defense budget, note that there can be a large difference between budget authorizations, budget appropriations, and the amount of actual government spending by definition. Table 5.3 notes the difference between spending authority and spending appropriations for fiscal year 2008.

As the table indicates, there can be large differences between actual and approved program spending for a given year. The table also shows where defense spending is concentrated. Operations and maintenance (salaries for civilian DoD employees, training, and maintenance), procurement (equipment purchases), and military personnel (active duty salaries) are the three largest categories, each with over $120 billion in funding in fiscal year 2008.

Commodities   Like construction spending described in previous pages, commodities are driven by economic growth and are a major

Table 5.3   Fiscal Year 2008 US Defense Authority vs. Appropriation Spending (In $)

Program	Authority*	Appropriation*	Difference*
Operation & Maintenance	$222.3	$217.7	$4.6
Procurement	$126.2	$115.4	$10.8
Military Personnel	$120.3	$121.2	−$0.9
RDT&E**	$76.5	$74.4	$2.1
Military Construction	$17.8	$10.2	$7.6
Revolving & Mgmt Funds	$3.7	$2.1	$1.6
Family Housing	$2.9	$4.3	−$1.4
Total	$569.7	$545.3	$24.4

*All values in $ billions.
**Research Testing Development and Evaluation
Source: US Department of Defense.

driver for Industrials firms. Finding free online data is a challenge for non-professional analysts, but limited data can be found on the websites of certain commodity exchanges. The London Metal Exchange (www.lme.co.uk) provides free metals pricing for one calendar year, and the New York Mercantile Exchange (www.nymex.com) provides commodity futures and options data both intraday and historically.

Architecture Billings Index   The American Institute of Architects (AIA) "Work-on-the-Boards" billings index is a good leading indicator of nonresidential construction activity, as evidenced in Figure 5.2. The left-hand axis shows the percent change of monthly private, nonresidential construction spending compared to the same month the year prior, while the right-hand axis is the monthly Architectural Billings Index number lagged by nine months.

Each month, the AIA surveys its members and determines whether billings have increased significantly (greater than 5 percent), decreased significantly (greater than 5 percent), or something in between relative to the previous month. The AIA aggregates the monthly survey and creates an index by adding up the percent of firms reporting a significant

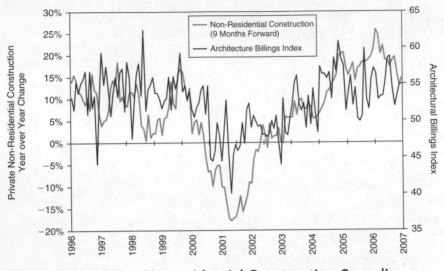

Figure 5.2 ABI vs. Nonresidential Construction Spending
Source: Bloomberg Finance L.P.

increase in activity and the half of the total of the firms reporting no change. Any mark above 50 denotes growth. The data can be found on the AIA's website (www.aia.org).

What About International Indicators?

How can you best gauge how well international markets are doing? The OECD (www.oecd. org) makes it easy. The group provides a wide range of economic metrics like GDP, industrial production, business confidence, and gross fixed capital formation for its 30 member nations. The OECD also lists the website for each country's data office and provides links to other international organization data sources at http://stats.oecd.org/source.

Measuring Corporate Health

While there are many ways to gauge economic strength, measuring corporate health for the broad market can be challenging because it requires analysis of multiple sources, none of which is perfect or gives a complete perspective. Further, just because a firm is healthy financially doesn't necessarily mean it will purchase new equipment and/or help spur growth for Industrials.

There are a few ways one can gauge the financial health of the broad market. This includes company earnings announcements, news stories, and the BEA corporate profit report.

Company Earnings Announcements   Investors can evaluate end-market conditions via company earnings announcements in one of two ways. The first is reading through Industrials firms' earnings announcements and company SEC filings because they typically provide commentary on their end markets including information on customer spending expectations and product demand. Investors can also evaluate end-market fundamentals themselves to determine if future spending is likely. This often requires analysis of firms outside the Industrials sector.

Firms will typically hold quarterly analyst conference calls to explain their results and answer any questions. The transcript of these calls can usually be found online or on the firm's investor relations page. Earnings information can also be found on the Filings and Forms section of the SEC website (www.sec.gov). Domestic companies file their "10-Q" for their quarterly earnings announcement and "10-K" for their annual report. Selected foreign firms who have shares listed in the US will file a "20-F," which is the annual report for a foreign company.

News Sources   There are many good news sources that can help in monitoring the Industrials sector and its end markets. The *Wall Street Journal* (www.wsj.com), the *Financial Times* (www.ft.com), and Bloomberg (www.bloomberg.com/) are among the most popular for finance news. These sites, as well as commonly used ones like Reuters (www.reuters.com), *BusinessWeek* (www.businessweek.com), and Business Wire (www.businesswire.com), allow you to screen news by industry.

Corporate Profit Reports   The BEA (www.bea.gov) releases quarterly US corporate profits with its GDP report. The report breaks down profits by industry, which is helpful when analyzing end markets and their propensity to spend on Industrials' equipment and services moving forward. While increasing corporate profits is not a requirement for future spending, it's often an encouragement.

Monitoring Access to Cheap Capital

The ease and cost of borrowing is an important factor for a firm deciding to purchase new equipment. A number of online sources report applicable interest rates like corporate bond rates, mortgage rates, government bond rates, and yield curves.

Interest Rates The Federal Reserve (www.federalreserve.com) reports daily yields on a number of financial instruments including commercial paper, Treasury bills and bonds, and corporate bonds of varying duration. One can also find current government bond yields and yield curves for large countries on Bloomberg's website, and US mortgage rates at www.bankrate.com.

Equipment Leasing and Finance Association's (ELFA) Monthly Leasing and Finance Index ELFA (www.elfaonline.org) produces the Monthly Leasing and Finance Index (MLFI-25), which reflects financing conditions for investing in US capital equipment. The report reflects financing conditions based on survey results for all capital equipment (including goods manufactured outside of Industrials) and all forms of financing (including lines of credit, leases, and term loans).

The monthly report is broken into five components—New Business Volume, Aging of Receivables, Average Losses, Capital Approval Ratios, and Total Number of Employees—each providing a glimpse into a different facet of the capital equipment finance market.

- **New business volume.** Value in USD billions of new financing volumes. Monthly data and the monthly change year-over-year is highlighted.

- **Aging of receivables.** Percent of all account receivables that are over 30 days old. Account receivables are money owed to a company where a good has been sold but payment has not been received.
- **Average losses (charge-offs) as a percentage of net receivables.** Percentage of the amount of receivables management believes will never be recovered to total net receivables (account receivables minus bad debts).
- **Credit approval ratios as percentage of all decisions submitted.** Approved financing as a percentage of all requests submitted.
- **Total number of employees.** Total headcount for the equipment finance business.

Loan Survey   The Federal Reserve (www.federalreserve.gov) conducts a quarterly Senior Loan Officer Opinion Survey on Bank Lending Practices, which helps gauge how easily corporations and individuals are obtaining loans. Each quarter, the Federal Reserve surveys approximately 60 large domestic banks and 24 US branches of foreign banks to determine how lending standards, loan terms, and lending demand are changing. The report provides a good summary about the state of the lending market and is useful in gauging the ease, demand, and cost of accessing capital. Historically, inflation-adjusted, year-over-year GDP growth has been negatively correlated to tightening lending standards.

INDUSTRY SPECIFIC INDICATORS

Government reports and economic statistics are not the only way to evaluate fundamentals of the Industrials sector. Both the Capital Goods and Transportation Industry Groups have additional specific metrics helpful in analyzing these types of firms.

Capital Goods

For the Capital Goods industry group, investors may find *monthly machine orders*—released by a number of Capital Goods firms—a useful stat for analyzing market strength. For example, Caterpillar produces a monthly report highlighting three-month rolling orders for different regions, as shown in Table 5.4.

A number of other US firms produce similar metrics to aid in your investment analysis, including the following (industries in parenthesis):

- **Boeing** (Aerospace & Defense)—www.boeing.com
- **Emerson Electric** (Electrical Equipment)—www.emersonelectric.com
- **Deere** (Machinery)—www.deere.com
- **Fastenal** (Trading Companies & Distributors)—www.fastenal.com
- **Grainger** (Trading Companies & Distributors)—www.grainger.com
- **Illinois Tool Works** (Machinery)—www.itwinc.com
- **Parker-Hannifin** (Machinery)—www.parker.com

The releases generally provide both regional and major product breakdowns useful in analyzing and comparing different markets.

Transportation Industry

Like Capital Goods industries, there are numerous metrics to monitor and evaluate Transportation industries. These metrics are relatively timely and provide a good way to monitor how transportation industries are performing. Commonly used metrics include:

- Railroad volumes
- Cargo volumes
- The truck tonnage index
- Shipping rates
- Airline traffic data

Rail Volumes   The Association of American Railroads (www.aar.org) publishes a weekly summary of freight railroad volumes. The data are

Table 5.4 2007 Machine Dealer Reported Retail Statistics

Period Ended	Asia/Pacific	EAME*	Latin America	Subtotal	North America	World
January	21%	27%	0%	20%	−9%	4%
February	10%	32%	1%	19%	−10%	3%
March	20%	43%	25%	32%	−15%	6%
April	16%	32%	29%	27%	−14%	4%
May	23%	35%	15%	27%	−13%	4%
June	12%	27%	−1%	17%	−13%	−1%
July	16%	32%	−5%	19%	−14%	1%
August	10%	27%	0%	17%	−9%	3%
September	16%	26%	3%	19%	−12%	3%
October	16%	25%	21%	22%	−14%	4%
November	23%	31%	49%	32%	−15%	9%
December	19%	24%	70%	30%	−13%	9%

Source: Caterpillar.[3]
*Europe, Africa, and Middle East

useful in monitoring railroads and US shipping demand. The data are broken down by product type, both weekly and cumulative year-to-date, which helps in evaluating end markets as well.

Cargo Volumes   The Bureau of Transportation Statistics (www.bts.gov) releases air cargo volumes monthly—useful when analyzing Air Freight & Logistics firms and airlines. The report breaks down volumes by region and can be broken down by airline. Similarly, the International Air Transport Association (www.iata.org) reports international freight volumes (domestic volumes are excluded) broken down by region of origin.

Truck Tonnage Index   Similar to the rail volumes statistics produced by the American Association of Railroads, the American Trucking Association (ATA) produces the truck tonnage index (www.truckline.com) monthly, which can be used as a proxy for US trucking demand. The ATA conducts member surveys to determine the total weight of their monthly tonnage. The responses are aggregated, manipulated, and placed into two indexes—one seasonally adjusted, and one non-seasonally adjusted.

Shipping Rates   The Baltic Dry Freight Index, the most widely cited shipping-rate index, is a compilation of shipping rates across four different ship sizes (based on their dead weight tons capacity) and 26 different shipping routes aggregated by the Baltic Exchange (www.balticexchange.com).

Although not all shipping rates are based off the Baltic Freight Index, the index is a good way to monitor the strength of the Marine industry. The Baltic Freight Index value can be accessed via Bloomberg's website (www.bloomberg.com).

Airline Traffic Data   Monitoring airline traffic data is useful in determining the strength of the airline industry. Domestic airline traffic data can be found on the Bureau of Transportation's website (www.bts.gov) and international traffic data can be found on the International Air Transport Association's website (www.iata.org).

Chapter Recap

Commonly used metrics and statistics can be useful in tracking the fundamentals of the Industrials sector and its major end markets. A good understanding of these metrics will provide an analyst a thorough view of the sector and the tools necessary to making better, forward-looking Industrials investment decisions.

- Economic statistics do not provide a crystal ball, but they are helpful in understanding the sector and shaping future expectations.
- Industrials are economically sensitive, making economic metrics like GDP and business cycle indicators important.
- A large percentage of the Industrials sector are manufacturers, which makes manufacturing-based metrics like durable goods, ISM manufacturing numbers, and industrial production important to follow.
- End markets like construction, defense, commodities, and manufacturing can all be monitored by economic statistics and online data providers.
- Monthly sales orders and transportation statistics make tracking Capital Goods and Transportation industries easier.

THE INFRASTRUCTURE MARKET

A recurring theme in Industrials sector analysis is the importance of government spending, specifically as it relates to infrastructure-related industries. This chapter examines more closely Industrials' role in infrastructure and how investors can profit. Infrastructure literally provides the highways and byways for an economy and society to function and grow—whether it's power plants, roads, phone lines, and so on. These structures can create powerful primary and secondary benefits to its users and society as a whole. For example, a new road facilitates the transport of goods. But with road construction also comes many important secondary benefits like increases in productivity associated with quicker travel times, reduced emissions, and increased gas savings.

These roads, power plants, and phone lines provide the necessary foundations for economic growth to occur. Ronald M. DeFeo, Terex chairman and chief executive officer, captured it correctly when he said, "Fundamentally, infrastructure investment equals economic prosperity, they are attached at the hip."[1]

Infrastructure crosses many industries but can be broken down into five main categories:

1. **Energy.** Electric power generation, transmission, and distribution, and natural gas transmission and distribution.
2. **Social.** Universities, schools, hospitals, prisons, sports stadiums, public housing, and community facilities.
3. **Telecommunications.** Fixed and mobile phone lines, Internet, cable networks, satellite, television, and radio towers.
4. **Transport.** Airport runways and terminals, railways, toll roads, bridges, highways, tunnels, ports, logistics centers, and other transit systems.
5. **Water and Sanitation.** Potable water generation and distribution and sewage collection and treatment.

These are all very different markets, each with their own unique benefits and reasons for investment. But investment in all of them comes with large price tags, which is beneficial to Industrials, who often supplies the equipment and the construction services for this investment.

A VERY BIG MARKET

According to the World Bank, the value of the world's physical infrastructure (excluding housing and social facilities) was approximately $15 trillion as of 2000.[2] Table 6.1 shows the value is concentrated in electricity and roads, primarily in high- and middle-income nations. Notice the relative importance of water and sanitation is inversely related to income levels, while telecom investment typically increases as incomes rise.

A growing global economy means expectations for future infrastructure spending are large—a positive for many Industrials industries. Not only will developing nations require new infrastructure, but established economies have aging infrastructures requiring replacement as well. Just a few examples of recent estimates for needed infrastructure upgrades include:

Table 6.1 Infrastructure by Type and Income Group

Type	Low Income	Middle Income	High Income	World
Electricity	26%	48%	40%	40%
Roads	51%	28%	45%	41%
Water & Sanitation	15%	10%	5%	8%
Rail	7%	7%	4%	5%
Telecom (Fixed)	1%	3%	2%	3%
Telecom (Mobile)	1%	4%	4%	3%
Total ($ Billions)	$1,968	$4,194	$8,804	$14,966

Source: World Bank.[3]

- Global infrastructure investment could equal approximately $65 trillion by 2030.[4]
- Approximately $21.7 trillion will be spent on developing nations' infrastructure over the next decade.[5]
- Canada may require approximately $189 billion in public infrastructure investment to maintain the country's private-sector competitiveness.[6]
- Bringing US infrastructure to good condition may require as much as $2.2 trillion over the next five years.[7]

To counter such investment requirements, a number of countries initiated large infrastructure spending plans, including the following:

- China's 11th five-year plan calls for approximately $700 billion in infrastructure spending from 2006 through 2010.[8]
- In 2007, Mexico initiated its National Infrastructure Program (NIP), which calls for between $150 billion and $301 billion in infrastructure spending through 2012.[9]
- In 2008, Russia approved a $570 billion infrastructure program with funding primarily going for more roads, rails, and airports.[10]
- In 2008, Saudi Arabia announced that $800 billion would be invested in the country over the next 10 years.[11]
- In 2009, Brazil announced spending of $281 billion on infrastructure projects between 2007 and 2010, an increase from the $229 billion originally announced in 2007.[12]

INFRASTRUCTURE INVESTMENT DRIVERS

What's driving such large infrastructure spending expectations and requirements? Among the reasons are:

- Supporting economic growth
- Overusing aging infrastructure
- Growing urbanization
- Encouraging foreign direct investment (FDI)
- Ensuring public safety

Supporting Economic Growth

Nationally, transportation infrastructure—the development of roads and rail lines—integrates nations and expands markets for local companies. A nation's infrastructure allows production to leave congested cities to areas where land is more plentiful and potentially closer to natural resources. This development can also spur productivity gains as manufacturers are able to access new supplies and production bottlenecks are reduced.

Globally, infrastructure links a nation to the rest of the world. Telecommunication infrastructure enables data transfer, improves international communication, and helps foster new business relationships. Meanwhile, new port construction links a country or a region to the rest of the world by trade, expanding new market opportunities for imports and exports. These links only become more important as the global economy grows.

Increased and ongoing investment will also be needed because current infrastructure in many nations is becoming overburdened. Increased trade requires the expansion of port facilities and railroad capacity. Increased driving and use of cars drives demand for new roads, and growing industrialization increases demand for power and energy.

Overusing Aging Infrastructure

Aging infrastructure and years of under-investment in the US and Europe have led to outdated public resources as upgrades have not kept up with increased product demand. Roads have become increasingly congested, pipes are leaking, and power plants are having difficulty producing enough electricity to satiate demand. The results have proven costly, with hundreds of billions of dollars lost in congestion-related expenses and productivity.[13]

In 2009, the American Society of Civil Engineers (ASCE) issued their report card on the state of US infrastructure. Each category was evaluated on the basis of condition and performance, capacity versus need, and funding versus need. In total, the US received a "D" rating, with total investment needs estimated at $2.2 trillion. Table 6.2 provides a sampling of their grades.

Only one industry saw their grade improve from 2005 to 2009, and all industries received a score of "mediocre" or worse—this alone indicates the dire need for new infrastructure spending in the years ahead.

Growing Urbanization

The world is only becoming more urbanized and cities more congested, as evidenced in Figure 6.1. Data suggest this trend will continue,

Table 6.2   Infrastructure Report Card

Subject	2005 Grade	2009 Grade
Aviation	D+	D
Bridges	C	C
Dams	D	D
Drinking Water	D–	D–
National Power Grid	D	D+
Hazardous Waste	D	D
Navigable Waterways	D–	D–
Road	D	D–
Schools	D	D
Solid Waste	C+	C+
Transit	D+	D
Wastewater	D–	D–

Source: American Society of Civil Engineers.

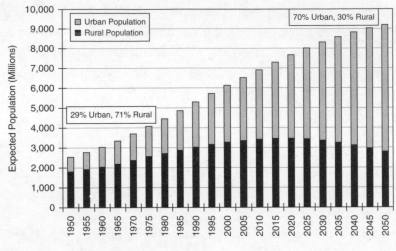

Figure 6.1   Growing Urbanization
Source: United Nations.

placing further strains on current infrastructure like roads, hospitals, public transportation, housing, and utilities.

The pending urbanization boom will require billions in spending to ensure current infrastructure is not overwhelmed by increased use.

Encouraging Foreign Direct Investment

Proper infrastructure, of particular issue in emerging markets, increases a nation's competitiveness in attracting foreign direct investment (FDI). Globalization has driven trillions in FDI as firms seek to establish local sales bases and capitalize on cheaper overseas labor. Globally, competition for this money is increasing, making adequate infrastructure systems that much more important. For some emerging markets, inadequate infrastructure is a major hindrance in attracting FDI. Lack of infrastructure can limit investment while stunting economic growth, productivity, and future development.

Ensuring Public Safety

As infrastructure ages beyond its useful life, the risk of failure and malfunction increases, potentially putting the public at risk. In 2007, aging infrastructure and public safety were highlighted when a bridge collapsed in Minneapolis, killing 13 people and injuring another 145. Only a month prior, a steam pipe installed in 1924 exploded in New York City, killing one and injuring another 30.

On Shaky Ground

According to the US Federal Highway Administration, over 25 percent of US bridges in 2007 were considered "structurally deficient" or "obsolete," down from over 31 percent in 1996. Be careful driving in Washington DC, Rhode Island, and Massachusetts: More than 50 percent of bridges in these states and district received the deficient and obsolete tag in 2007.

Source: US Federal Highway Administration.

RISKS TO INFRASTRUCTURE GROWTH

Though it may seem that future spending on infrastructure is inevitable, there are risks to its growth, given the complexity of creating these structures and the political, financial, and execution difficulties that can arise with multi-billion dollar projects. The primary risks we cover include:

- **Economic and government.** Bureaucracy, corruption, deteriorating budget conditions, allocation of money to social initiatives, and lack of public support.
- **Execution.** Labor shortages, commodity and machinery shortages, and cost overrides and increases.
- **Financial market.** Difficulty raising funds and financial market conditions.

Economic and Government Risks

Future infrastructure spending will be predicated on global economic health and the overall success of governments in power. Particularly in emerging markets, bureaucracy and corruption can limit growth.

Project delays are common. As Michael W. Sutherlin, CEO and president of US machinery producer Joy Global, noted in the company's fiscal first quarter 2008 earnings conference call, "The government in India continues to promise great things, but they have promised great things for a long time and [are] always slow to deliver. There is a lot of bureaucracy [that] gets in the way."[14] Not surprisingly, "inefficient government bureaucracy" ranks in the top five of the most problematic factors for a number of emerging markets including Brazil, Russia, India, China, Indonesia, and Mexico.[15]

Deteriorating budget conditions can also impact optimistic government spending plans as falling tax revenues and government profits limit available funds. Metal prices and export growth saw significant run-ups between 2003 and 2007 that helped goad commodity-rich and export-focused emerging market economies to fund their infrastructure programs. And while strength during this period led to ambitious infrastructure spending plans, there is no certainty economic conditions will remain as favorable moving forward.

Execution Risks

Project execution is always a risk, especially when resources like labor, machinery, and raw materials are limited. This scarcity, coupled with increasingly complex infrastructure projects and escalating costs, can easily lead to projects going over budget and/or not getting completed.

Large, multi-million dollar facilities are prime candidates for cost overrides, as South Africa discovered. In 2008, Danny Jordaan, chief executive of the local organizing committee of the 2010 World Cup, told reporters that cost overruns on stadiums for the 2010 World Cup would be over $300 million due to various factors including the weakening South African rand, increased steel and cement prices, striking employees, and complexities in project designs.[16] Future funding to make up the shortfall is not guaranteed and cost increases can significantly impair contractor profitability. This should be monitored for any individual Construction & Engineering industry firm.

Financial Market Risks

The large costs associated with these infrastructure projects can also put strains on government and corporate budgets, especially if borrowing costs rise and project profitability is reduced. This is especially true for projects typically financed through issuing bonds. Corporations' inability to access money—whether via the capital markets, private placements, or bank loans—will also limit investment and infrastructure needs.

Financial market risks may also affect the individual contractors responsible for the projects should they encounter their own difficulties raising capital for capital expenditure spending and to fund expansions.

PARTICIPATING IN THE INFRASTRUCTURE BOOM

How can investors translate a potential boom in infrastructure investment to portfolio profits? There are three primary vehicles:

1. Participating in public private partnerships (PPP).
2. Buying exchange traded funds (ETF) and mutual funds.
3. Buying infrastructure-related stocks.

Public Private Partnerships

Public-private partnerships (PPP) are agreements allowing private companies to design, construct, and operate infrastructure projects that have historically been operated by the government. While multiple PPP arrangements exist, most basically entail some form of private capital or government funding, construction, operation, and/or the maintenance of an infrastructure project, and government payment in return.

While still monitored and regulated by the government, PPPs allow private enterprises to gain access to new market opportunities. Among the many benefits for governments, PPPs remove the infrastructure financial strain from government budgets and allow new sources of capital, market expertise, and labor to enter the market.

Unlike the government, these contractors are profit-driven and often leaders within their respective industries, bringing advanced technical abilities that can lower project costs, decrease project construction time, mitigate project risks, and increase project quality. This has a limited impact to public resources and finances. The Pennsylvania Turnpike, Florida's Alligator Alley, and Chicago's Skyway Toll Road are run under this sort of arrangement.

Taking Its Toll

Japan has one of the largest toll-road networks in the world (5,717 miles). Nearly two-thirds of the 7,891 miles of trunk roads and expressways are tolled. This compares to the 4,744 miles within the US National Highway System (NHS)—approximately 3 percent of total highway miles.

Source: OECD; the Federal Highway Administration.

To tap this market, a number of asset managers, private equity firms, and Transportation Infrastructure firms have created new global infrastructure funds to invest in these infrastructure projects. Typically, a group of investors will create a partnership to bid on PPP projects. The winning bidder then borrows money to finance the project's construction, which gets paid back through fees and payments from the government. Any revenues in excess of project costs are profits for investors. These contracts are typically long term—sometimes upward of 20 to 50 years. Infrastructure investing is considered an alternative investment class that can provide investors uncorrelated returns to the global markets, stable long-term cash flows, and inflation protection.

Figure 6.2 shows investment activity increasing through most of the decade. (The line shows number of deals, and the bars show total deal value in billions.) The market value of infrastructure purchases increased 320 percent from 2004 through 2008. While these infrastructure funds are not the only industries that participate in PPPs, they are major purchasers of infrastructure assets.

Generally speaking, the US PPP market has had difficulty gaining traction relative to foreign markets as fears of private and potentially

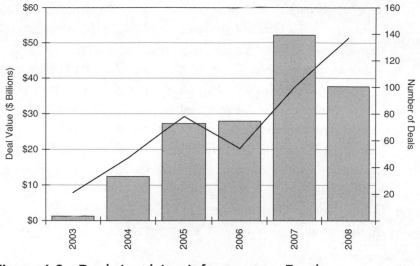

Figure 6.2   Deals Involving Infrastructure Funds
Source: Thomson Reuters.

foreign enterprises managing US infrastructure have led to national security and price gouging concerns. Port operator DP World, a subsidiary of government-owned Dubai World, encountered these fears firsthand in 2005 when it purchased the port management business at six major US seaports. After months of congressional debate regarding national security concerns, the House Committee on Appropriations voted 62–2 to block the deal and DP World agreed to sell its stake in the US ports to American International Group's asset-management business. As the ruling suggested, national security concerns can trump financial incentives to increase the size of the PPP market.

ETFs and Mutual Funds

There are a number of exchange-traded funds (ETFs) and mutual funds available to investors looking to gain exposure to the infrastructure market. They include:

- **Broad-based exposure.** iShares Infrastructure Fund (IGF), the SPDR FTSE/Macquarie Global Infrastructure Fund (GII), Macquarie Global Infrastructure Total Return Fund Inc

(MGU), First American Global Infrastructure (FGIAX), Cohen & Steers Global Infrastructure Fund (CSUAX), and the Kensington Global Infrastructure Fund (KGIAX).

- **Water exposure.** PowerShares Water Resources (PHO), First Trust ISE Water Index (FIW), Claymore S&P Global Water Index (CGW), and the PowerShares Global Water Portfolio (PIO).
- **Energy exposure.** Market Vectors Nuclear Energy (NLR), Macquarie/First Trust Global Infrastructure/Utilities Dividend & Income Fund (MFD), and the Tortoise Energy Infrastructure Fund (TYG).
- **Other.** PowerShares Building & Construction (PKB) and the Mark Vectors Environmental Services (EVX).

As new ETFs and mutual funds are constantly being added to the market, it's best to research all product offerings before investing. Websites such as www.etfguide.com are useful tools for researching current ETF options.

Buying Infrastructure-Related Stocks

Investors can also benefit from the infrastructure theme by buying individual stocks. Focus on the end market you would like to capture (e.g., port infrastructure, toll roads, power generation, building construction, etc.), and then find the companies most attractive in that group (see Chapter 8 for more on how to select stocks). Industrials industries to focus on include:

- **Construction & Engineering.** Design, engineering, and construction of new infrastructure projects.
- **Electrical Products.** Power generation equipment and the creation of alternative energy sources like wind turbines and solar power.
- **Industrial Conglomerates.** Mixed exposure given the diversity of the industry; products include power generation equipment, wind turbines, water purification systems, and medical equipment.

- **Machinery.** Road paving equipment and heavy machinery used in infrastructure construction.
- **Transportation Infrastructure.** Developer and operator of infrastructure projects.

Another way to find firms leveraged to infrastructure is to search through news stories and company conference call transcripts.

Investors can evaluate the success of their infrastructure projects by comparing their results to infrastructure-related indexes like the Dow Jones Brookfield Global Infrastructure Index and the S&P Global Infrastructure Index. Both are global infrastructure-related funds that own companies leveraged to the infrastructure markets. Monitoring these indexes will help investors understand how well the industry is performing as a whole and get a sense of market perception surrounding the infrastructure theme.

Chapter Recap

Infrastructure is the foundation of economic growth and development. It promotes productivity, enables modernization, and increases global connectivity. And while not without risk, the market provides important gains to an economy and numerous market opportunities for investors.

- Supporting economic growth, fixing aging infrastructure, growing urbanization, encouraging foreign direct investment, and ensuring public safety are among the important drivers of infrastructure investment.
- Risks include project execution, financial market concerns, and government bureaucracy leading to significant cost increases and potentially derailing infrastructure projects.
- An investor can participate in the infrastructure market by purchasing infrastructure-related ETFs, transportation infrastructure companies, or companies operationally exposed to the market.

III

THINKING LIKE A
PORTFOLIO MANAGER

7

THE TOP-DOWN METHOD

If you're bullish on Industrials, how much of your portfolio should you put in Industrials stocks? Twenty-five percent? Fifty? One hundred percent? This question concerns portfolio management. Most investors concern themselves only with individual companies ("I like Caterpillar, so I'll buy some") without considering how they fit into their overall portfolio. But this is no way to manage your money.

In this part of the book, we show you how to analyze Industrials companies like a top-down portfolio manager. This includes a full description of the top-down method, how to use benchmarks, and how the top-down method applies to the Industrials sector. We then delve into security analysis in Chapter 8, where we provide a framework for analyzing any company, and then discuss many of the important questions to ask when analyzing Industrials companies. Finally, in Chapter 9, we conclude by giving a few examples of specific investing strategies for the Industrials sector.

INVESTING IS A SCIENCE

Too many investors today think investing has "rules"—that all one must do to succeed in investing for the long run is find the right set of investing rules. But that simply doesn't work. Why? All well-known and widely discussed information is already reflected in stock prices. This is a basic tenet of market theory and commonly referred to as *market efficiency*. So if you see a headline about a stock you follow, there's no use trading on that information—it's already priced in. You missed the move.

If everything known is already discounted in prices, the only way to consistently beat the market is to know something others don't. Think about it: There are many intelligent investors and long-time professionals who fail to beat the market year after year—most with the same access to information as anyone, if not more. Why?

Most view investing as a craft. They think, "If I learn the craft of value investing and all its rules, then I can be a successful investor using that method." But that simply can't work because, by definition, all the conventional ways of thinking about value investing will already be widely known and thus priced in. In fact, most investment styles are very well known and already widely practiced. There are undoubtedly millions of investors out there much like you, looking at the same metrics and information you are. So there isn't much power in them. Even the investing techniques themselves are widely known—taught to millions in universities and practiced by hundreds of thousands of professionals globally. There's no edge.

Moreover, it's been demonstrated investment styles move in and out of favor over time—no one style or category is inherently better than another in the long run. You may think "value" investing works wonders to beat markets, but the fact is growth stocks will trounce value at times.

The key to beating stock markets lies in being dynamic—never adhering to a single investment idea all the time—and gleaning information the market hasn't yet priced in. In other words, you cannot adhere to a single set of "rules" and hope to outperform markets over time.

So how can you beat the markets? By thinking of investing as a science.

EINSTEIN'S BRAIN AND THE STOCK MARKET

If he weren't so busy becoming the most renowned scientist of the twentieth century, Albert Einstein would have made a killing on Wall

Street—but not because he had such a high IQ. Granted, he was immensely intelligent, but a high IQ alone does not make a market guru. (If it did, MIT professors would be making millions managing money instead of teaching.) Instead, it's the style of his thought and the method of his work that matter.

From the little we know about Einstein's investment track record, he didn't do very well. He lost most of his Nobel Prize money in bad bond ventures.[1] Heck, Sir Isaac Newton may have given us the three laws of motion, but even his talents didn't extend to investing. He lost his shirt in the South Sea Bubble of the early 1700s, explaining later, "I can calculate the movement of the stars, but not the madness of men."

So why believe Einstein would have been a great portfolio manager if he put his mind to it? In short, Einstein was a true and highly creative scientist. He didn't take the acknowledged rules of physics as such—he used prior knowledge, logic, and creativity, combined with the rigors of the verifiable, testable scientific method, to create an entirely new view of the cosmos. In other words, he was dynamic and gleaned knowledge others didn't have. Investors must do the same. (Not to worry, you won't need advanced calculus to do it.)

Einstein's unique character gave him an edge—he truly had a mind made to beat markets. Scientists have perused his work, his speeches, his letters, even his brain (literally) to find the secret of his intellect. In all, his approach to information processing and idea generation, his willingness to go against the grain of the establishment, and his relentless pursuit of answers to questions no one else was asking during his time ultimately made him a genius.

Both his contemporaries and most biographers agree one of Einstein's foremost gifts was his ability to discern "the big picture." Unlike many scientists who could easily drown themselves in data minutiae, Einstein had an ability to see above the fray. Another way to say this is he could take the same information everyone else at his time was looking at and interpret it differently, yet correctly. He accomplished this using his talent for extracting the most important data from what he studied and linking them together in innovative ways no one else could.

Einstein called this "combinatory play." Similar to a child experimenting with a new Lego set, Einstein would combine and recombine seemingly unrelated ideas, concepts, and images to produce new, original discoveries. In the end, most all new ideas are merely the combination of existing ones in one form or another. Take $E = mc^2$: Einstein was not the first to discover the concepts of energy, mass, or the speed of light; rather, he combined these concepts in a novel way and, in the process, altered the way in which we view the universe.[2]

Einstein's combinatory play is a terrific metaphor for stock investing. To be a successful market strategist, you must be able to extract the most important data from all of the "noise" permeating today's markets and generate conclusions the market hasn't yet appreciated. Central to this task is your ability to link data together in unique ways and produce new insights and themes for your portfolio in the process.

Einstein learned science basics just like his peers. But once he had those mastered he directed his brain to challenging prior assumptions and inventing entirely different lenses to look through.

This is why this book isn't intended to give you a "silver bullet" for picking the right Industrials stocks. The fact is the "right" Industrials stocks will be different in different times and situations. You don't have to be Einstein, you just have to think differently—and like a scientist—if you want to beat markets.

THE TOP-DOWN METHOD

Overwhelmingly, investment professionals today do what can broadly be labeled "bottom-up" investing. Their emphasis is stock selection. A typical bottom-up investor researches an assortment of companies and attempts to pick those with the greatest likelihood of outperforming the market based on individual merits. The selected securities are cobbled together to form a portfolio, and factors like country and economic sector exposures are purely residuals of security selection, not planned decisions.

"Top-down" investing reverses the order. A top-down investor first analyzes big picture factors like economics, politics, and sentiment to forecast which investment categories are most likely to outperform the market. Only then does a top-down investor begin looking at individual securities. Top-down investing is inevitably more concerned with a portfolio's aggregate exposure to investment categories than with any individual security. Thus, top-down is an inherently *dynamic* mode of investment because investment strategies are based upon the prevailing market and economic environment (which changes often).

There's significant debate in the investment community as to which approach is superior. This book's goal is not to reject bottom-up investing—there are indeed investors who've successfully utilized bottom-up approaches. Rather, the goal is to introduce a comprehensive and flexible methodology that any investor could use to build a portfolio designed to beat the global stock market in any investment environment. It's a framework for gleaning new insights and making good on information not already reflected in stock prices.

Before we describe the method, let's explore several key reasons why a top-down approach is advantageous:

- **Scalability.** A bottom-up process is akin to looking for needles in a haystack. A top-down process is akin to seeking the haystacks with the highest concentration of needles. Globally, there are nearly 25,000+ publicly traded stocks. Even the largest institutions with the greatest research resources cannot hope to adequately examine all these companies. Smaller institutions and individual investors must prioritize where to focus their limited resources. Unlike a bottom-up process, a top-down process makes this gargantuan task manageable by determining, up front, what slices of the market to examine at the security level.
- **Enhanced stock selection.** Well-designed top-down processes generate insights that can greatly enhance stock selection. Macro-economic or political analysis, for instance, can help determine what types of strategic attributes will face head or tailwinds (see Chapter 8 for a full explanation).
- **Risk control.** Bottom-up processes are highly subject to unintended risk concentrations. Top-down processes are inherently

better suited to manage risk exposures throughout the investment process.

- **Macro overview.** Top-down processes are more conducive to
avoiding macro-driven calamities like the bursting of the Japan
bubble in the 1990s, the Technology bubble in 2000, or the bear
market of 2000 to 2002. No matter how good an individual company may be, it is still beholden to sector, regional, and broader
market factors. In fact, there is evidence "macro" factors can largely
determine a stock's performance regardless of individual merit.

Top-Down Means Thinking 70-20-10

A top-down investment process also helps focus on what's most important to investment results: asset allocation and sub-asset allocation
decisions. Many investors focus most of their attention on security-
level portfolio decisions, like picking individual stocks they think will
perform well. However, studies have shown that over 90 percent of
return variability is derived from asset allocation decisions, not market
timing or stock selection.[3]

*Our research shows about 70 percent of return variability is derived
from asset allocation, 20 percent from sub-asset allocation (such as country, sector, size, and style), and 10 percent from security selection.* While
security selection can make a significant difference over time, higher-
level portfolio decisions dominate investment results more often
than not.

The balance of this chapter defines the various steps in the top-
down method, specifically as they relate to making country, sector,
and style decisions. This same basic framework can be applied to portfolios to make allocations within sectors. At the end of the chapter, we
detail how this framework can be applied to the Industrials sector.

Benchmarks

A key part of the top-down model is using benchmarks. A benchmark is typically a broad-based index of securities such as the S&P
500, MSCI World, or Russell 2000. Benchmarks are indispensible

roadmaps for structuring a portfolio, monitoring risk, and judging performance over time.

Tactically, a portfolio should be structured to maximize the probability of consistently beating the benchmark. This is inherently different than maximizing returns. Unlike aiming to achieve some fixed rate of return each year, which will cause disappointment when capital markets are very strong and is potentially unrealistic when the capital markets are very weak, a properly benchmarked portfolio provides a realistic guide for dealing with uncertain market conditions.

Portfolio construction begins by evaluating the characteristics of the chosen benchmark: sector weights, country weights, and market cap and valuations. Then an expected risk and return is assigned to each of these segments (based on portfolio drivers), and the most attractive areas are overweighted, while the least attractive are underweighted. Table 7.1 shows MSCI World benchmark sector characteristics as of December 31, 2008 as an example, while Table 7.2 shows country characteristics, and Table 7.3 shows market cap and valuations.

Table 7.1   MSCI World Characteristics—Sectors

Sector	Weight
Financials	18.6%
Health Care	11.9%
Energy	11.6%
Consumer Staples	11.1%
Industrials	10.9%
Information Technology	10.2%
Consumer Discretionary	8.9%
Materials	5.8%
Utilities	5.7%
Telecommunication	5.3%

Source: Thomson Datastream; MSCI, Inc.[4] as of 12/31/08.

Table 7.2   MSCI World Characteristics—Countries

Country	Weight
USA	49.7%
Japan	11.7%
UK	9.2%
France	5.1%
Germany	4.1%
Switzerland	3.9%
Canada	3.9%
Australia	2.8%
Spain	2.1%
Italy	1.7%
Netherlands	1.1%
Sweden	0.9%
Hong Kong	0.9%
Finland	0.6%
Singapore	0.5%
Denmark	0.4%
Belgium	0.3%
Norway	0.3%
Greece	0.2%
Portugal	0.2%
Austria	0.1%
Ireland	0.1%
New Zealand	0.0%
Emerging Markets	0.0%

Source: Thomson Datastream; MSCI, Inc.[5] as of 12/31/08.

Based on benchmark characteristics, portfolio drivers are then used to determine country, sector, and style decisions for the portfolio. For example, in Table 7.1 the Financials sector weight of the MSCI World Index is about 19 percent. Therefore, a portfolio managed against this benchmark would consider a 19 percent weight in

Table 7.3   MSCI World Characteristics—Market Cap and Valuations

	Valuations
Median Market Cap	$4.9 Billion
Weighted Average Market Cap	$57.4 Billion
P/E	9.7
P/B	1.7
Div Yield	3.8
P/CF	14.5
P/S	1.6
Number of Holdings	1693

Notes: P/E = price-earnings ratio; P/B = price-to-book ratio; Div Yield = dividend yield; P/CF = price-to-cash-flow ratio; P/S = price-to-sales ratio.

Source: Thomson Datastream; MSCI, Inc.[6] as of 12/31/08.

Financials "neutral," or market-weighted. If you believe Financials will perform better than the market in the foreseeable future, then you would "overweight" the sector, or hold more than 19 percent of your portfolio in Financials stocks. The reverse is true for an "underweight"—you'd hold less than 19 percent in Financials if you were pessimistic on the sector looking ahead.

Note that being pessimistic on Financials *doesn't necessarily mean holding zero Financials stocks.* It might only mean holding a lesser percentage of stocks in your portfolio than the benchmark. This is an important feature of benchmarking—it allows an investor to make strategic decisions on sectors and countries but maintains diversification, thus managing risk more appropriately.

For the Industrials sector, we can use Industrials-specific benchmarks like the S&P 500 Industrials, MSCI World Industrials, or Russell 2000 Producer Durables indexes. The components of these benchmarks can then be evaluated at a more detailed level, such as industry weights. (For example, we broke out MSCI World industry and industry benchmark weights in Chapter 4.)

TOP-DOWN DECONSTRUCTED

The top-down method begins by first analyzing the macro environment. It asks the "big" questions like: Do you think stocks will go up or down in the next 12 months? If so, which countries or sectors should benefit most? Once you have decided on these high-level portfolio "drivers" (sometimes called "themes"), you can examine various macro portfolio drivers to make general overweight and underweight decisions for countries, sectors, industries, and sub-industries versus your benchmark.

For instance, let's say we've determined a macroeconomic driver that goes something like this: "In the next 12 months, I believe global infrastructure construction will be greater than most expect." That's a very high-level statement with important implications for your portfolio. It means you'd want to search for industries and, ultimately, stocks that would benefit most from increased infrastructure construction.

The second step in top-down is applying quantitative screening criteria to narrow the choice set of stocks. Since, in our hypothetical example, we believe infrastructure construction will be high, it likely means we're bullish on Machinery stocks. But which ones? Are you bullish on, say, heavy construction or light construction? Mining equipment producers? Agricultural equipment producers? Do you want producers with exposure to the US or another region? Do you want small-cap machinery companies or large cap? And what about valuations? Are you looking for growth or value? (Size and growth/value categories are often referred to as *style* decisions.) These criteria and more can help you narrow the list of stocks you might buy.

The third and final step is performing fundamental analysis on individual stocks. Notice that a great deal of thinking, analysis, and work is done before you ever think about individual stocks. That's the key to the top-down approach: It emphasizes high-level themes and funnels its way down to individual stocks, as illustrated in the following.

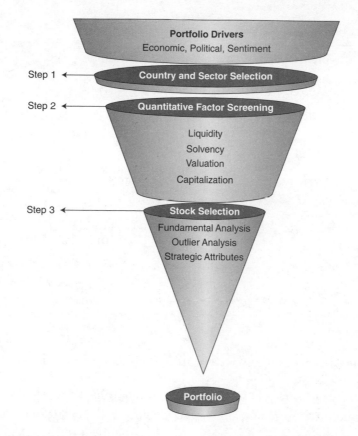

Step 1: Analyze Portfolio Drivers and Country and Sector Selection

Let's examine the first step in the top-down method more closely. In order to make top-down decisions, we develop and analyze what we call *portfolio drivers* (as mentioned previously). We segment these portfolio drivers in three general categories: *economic, political,* and *sentiment.*

Portfolio drivers are what drive the performance of a broad category of stocks. Accurately identifying current and future drivers will help you find areas of the market most likely to outperform or underperform your benchmark (i.e., the broader stock market).

Table 7.4 shows examples of each type of portfolio driver. It's important to note these drivers are by no means comprehensive nor

Table 7.4   Portfolio Drivers

Economic	Political	Sentiment
Yield curve spread	Taxation	Mutual fund flows
Relative GDP growth	Property rights	Relative style and asset class valuations
Monetary base/growth	Structural reform	Media coverage
Currency strength	Privatization	Institutional searches
Relative interest rates	Trade/capital barriers	Consumer confidence
Inflation	Current account	Foreign investment
Debt level (sovereign, corporate, consumer)	Government stability	Professional investor forecasts
Infrastructure spending	Political turnover	Momentum cycle analysis
M&A, issuance and repurchase activity	Wars/conflicts	Risk aversion

are they valid for all time periods. In fact, correctly identifying new portfolio drivers is essential to beating the market in the long term.

Economic Drivers   Economic drivers are anything related to the macroeconomic environment. This could include monetary policy, interest rates, lending activity, yield curve analysis, relative GDP growth analysis, and myriad others. What economic forces are likely to drive GDP growth throughout countries in the world? What is the outlook for interest rates and how would that impact sectors? What is the outlook for technology and infrastructure spending among countries?

Economic drivers pertain not only to the fundamental outlook of the economy (GDP growth, interest rates, inflation), but also to the stock market (valuations, M&A activity, share buybacks). As an investor, it's your job to identify these drivers and determine how they'll impact your overall portfolio and each of its segments.

The following is an example list of economic drivers that could impact portfolio performance:

- US economic growth will be higher than consensus expectations.
- European Union interest rates will remain benign.

- Mergers, acquisitions, and share buybacks will remain strong.
- Emerging markets growth will drive commodity demand.

Political Drivers Political drivers can be country specific, pertain to regions (the European Union, Organisation for Economic Cooperation and Development [OECD], etc.), or affect interaction between countries or regions (such as trade policies). These drivers are more concerned with categories such as taxation, government stability, fiscal policy, and political turnover. Which countries are experiencing a change in government that could have a meaningful impact on their economies? Which sectors could be at risk from new taxation or legislation? Which countries are undergoing pro-growth reforms?

Political drivers will help determine the relative attractiveness of market segments and countries based on the outlook for the political environment. Be warned, however: Most investors suffer from "home country bias," where they ascribe too much emphasis on the politics of their own country. Always keep in mind it's a big, interconnected world out there, and geopolitical developments everywhere can have implications.

What are possible political drivers you can find? Below is a list of examples that can drive stocks up or down.

- Political party change in Japan driving pro-growth reforms
- New tax policies in Germany stalling economic growth
- Protests, government coups, conflict driving political instability in Thailand

Sentiment Drivers Sentiment drivers attempt to measure consensus thinking about investment categories. Ideally, drivers identify market opportunities where sentiment is different than reality. For example, let's say you observe that current broad market sentiment expects a US recession in the next year. But you disagree and believe GDP growth will be strong. This presents an excellent opportunity for excess returns. You can load up on stocks that will benefit from an economic boom and watch the prices rise as the rest of the market realizes it much later.

Since the market is a discounter of all known information, it's important to try and identify what the market is pricing in. The interpretation of such investor drivers is typically counterintuitive (avoid what is overly popular and seek what is largely unpopular). Looking forward, which sectors are investors most bullish about and why? What countries or sectors are widely discussed in the media? What market segments have been bid up recently based on something other than fundamentals? If the market's perception is different than fundamentals in the short term, stocks will eventually correct themselves to reflect reality in the long term.

A note of caution: Gauging market sentiment does not mean being a *contrarian*. Contrarians are investors who simply do the opposite of what most believe will happen. Instead, find places where sentiment (people's beliefs) doesn't match what you believe is reality and over- or underweight sections of your portfolio accordingly, relative to your benchmark. Examples of sentiment drivers include:

- Investors remain pessimistic about Technology despite improving fundamentals.
- Sentiment for the Chinese stock market approaching euphoria, stretching valuations.
- Professional investors universally forecast US small-cap stocks to outperform.

How to Create Your Own Investment Drivers

In order to form your own investment drivers, the first step is accessing a wide array of data from multiple sources. For country drivers, this could range from globally focused publications like *The Wall Street Journal* or *Financial Times* to regional newspapers or government data. For sector drivers, this could include reading trade publications or following major company announcements.

Remember, however, that markets are efficient—they reflect all widely known information. Most pertinent information about public companies is, well, *public*. Which means the market already knows. News travels fast, and investor knowledge and expectations are absorbed by markets very quickly. Those seeking to profit on a bit of news, rumor, or speculation must acknowledge the market will probably move faster than they can. Therefore, in order to consistently generate excess returns, you must either know something others don't or interpret widely known information differently and correctly from the crowd. (For a detailed discussion on these factors and more, read *The Only Three Questions That Count* by Ken Fisher.)

Step 2: Quantitative Factor Screening

Step 2 in the top-down method is screening for quantitative factors. This allows you to narrow the potential list of stocks once your portfolio drivers are in place.

There are thousands and thousands of stocks out there, so it's vital to use a series of factors like market capitalization and valuations to narrow the field a bit. Securities passing this screen are then subjected to further quantitative analysis that eliminates companies with excessive risk profiles relative to their peer group, such as companies with excessive leverage or balance sheet risk and securities lacking sufficient liquidity for investment.

The rigidity of the quantitative screens is entirely up to you and will determine the number of companies on your prospect list. The more rigid the criteria, the fewer the companies that make the list. Broader criteria will increase the number of companies.

How can you perform such a screen? Here are two examples of quantitative factor screenings to show how broad, or specific, you can be. You might want to apply very strict criteria, or you may prefer to be broader.

Strict Criteria

- First, you decide you want to search for only Industrials firms. By definition, that excludes all companies from the other nine sectors. Already, you've narrowed the field a lot!
- Now, let's say that based on your high-level drivers you only want European Industrials stocks. By excluding all other regions besides Europe, you've narrowed the field even more.

- Next, let's decide to search only for Machinery firms in the Industrials sector.
- Perhaps you don't believe very small stocks are preferable, so you limit market capitalization to $5 billion and above.
- Lastly, let's set some parameters for valuation:
  - P/E (price to earnings) less than 13X
  - P/B (price to book) less than 4X
  - P/CF (price to cash flow) less than 11X
  - P/S (price to sales) less than 3X

This rigorous process of selecting parameters will yield a small number of stocks to research, all based on your higher-level themes. But maybe you have reason to be less specific and want to do a broader screen because you think Industrials in general is a good place to be.

Broad Criteria

- Industrials sector
- Global (no country or region restrictions)
- Market value above $10 billion

This selection process is much broader and obviously gives you a much longer list of stocks to choose from. Doing either a strict or broad screen isn't inherently better. It just depends on how well-formed and specific your higher-level themes are. Obviously, a stricter screen means less work for you in Step 3—actual stock selection.

Step 3: Stock Selection

After narrowing the prospect list, your final step is identifying individual securities possessing strategic attributes consistent with higher-level portfolio themes. (We'll cover the stock-selection process specifically in more detail in Chapter 8.) Your stock-selection process should attempt to accomplish two goals:

1. Find firms possessing strategic attributes consistent with higher-level portfolio themes, derived from the drivers that give those firms a competitive advantage versus their peers. For example,

if you believe owning firms with dominant market shares in consolidating industries is a favorable characteristic, you would search for firms with that profile.

2. Maximize the likelihood of beating the category of stocks you are analyzing. For example, if you want a certain portfolio weight of Machinery companies and need 4 stocks out of 12 meeting the quantitative criteria, then pick the 4 that, as a group, maximize the likelihood of beating all 12 as a whole. This is different than trying to pick "the best four." By avoiding stocks likely to be extreme or "weird" outliers versus the group, you can reduce portfolio risk while adding value at the security selection level.

In lieu of picking individual securities, there are other ways to exploit high-level themes in the top-down process. For instance, if you feel strongly about a particular industry but don't think you can add value through individual security analysis, it may be more prudent to buy a group of companies in the industry or via a category product like an exchange traded fund (ETF). There is a growing variety of ETFs that track the domestic and global Industrials sector, industries, and even thematic plays. This way, you can be sure to gain broad Industrials exposure without much stock-specific risk. (For more information on ETFs, visit www.ishares.com, www.sectorspdr .com, or www.masterdata.com.)

MANAGING AGAINST AN INDUSTRIALS BENCHMARK

Now we can practice translating this specifically to your Industrials allocation. Just as you analyze the components of your benchmark to determine country and sector components in a top-down strategy, you must analyze each sector's components, as we did in Chapter 4. To demonstrate how, we'll use the MSCI World Industrials Sector index as the benchmark. Table 7.5 shows the MSCI World Industrials industry weights as of December 31, 2008. We don't know what the sample portfolio weights should be, but we know it should add up to 100 percent. Of course, if managing against a broader benchmark, your Industrials sector weight may add up to more or less than the

Table 7.5   MSCI World Industrials Industry Weights vs. Sample Portfolio

Industry	MSCI World (%)	Sample Portfolio
Industrial Conglomerates	19.1%	?
Machinery	15.8%	?
Aerospace & Defense	15.1%	?
Road & Rail	11.0%	?
Electrical Equipment	8.9%	?
Air Freight & Logistics	5.6%	?
Construction & Engineering	5.6%	?
Commercial Services & Supplies	4.9%	?
Trading Companies & Distributors	4.5%	?
Building Products	2.5%	?
Professional Services	2.3%	?
Transportation Infrastructure	1.8%	?
Marine	1.6%	?
Airlines	1.3%	?
Total	100.0%	100%

Source: Thomson Datastream; MSCI, Inc.[7] as of 12/31/08.

Industrials weight in the benchmark, depending on over- or under-weight decisions.

Keeping the industry weights in mind will help mitigate benchmark risk. If you have a portfolio of stocks with the same industry weights as the MSCI World Industrials Index, you're *neutral*—taking no benchmark risk. However, if you feel strongly about an industry, like Transportation Infrastructure, and decide to only purchase those firms (one of the smallest weights in the sector), you're taking a huge benchmark risk. The same is true if you significantly *underweight* an industry. All the same rules apply when you do this from a broader portfolio perspective, as we did earlier in this chapter.

The benchmark's industry weights provide a jumping-off point in making further portfolio decisions. Once you make higher-level decisions on the industries, you can make choices versus the benchmark by overweighting the industries you feel will likely perform best and

Table 7.6   Portfolio A

Industry	MSCI World	Portfolio A	Difference
Industrial Conglomerates	19.1%	21.4%	2.3%
Machinery	15.8%	10.0%	−5.8%
Aerospace & Defense	15.1%	22.1%	7.0%
Road & Rail	11.0%	2.2%	−8.8%
Electrical Equipment	8.9%	9.8%	0.9%
Air Freight & Logistics	5.6%	4.3%	−1.3%
Construction & Engineering	5.6%	13.8%	8.2%
Commercial Services & Supplies	4.9%	2.4%	−2.5%
Trading Companies & Distributors	4.5%	0.0%	−4.5%
Building Products	2.5%	3.0%	0.5%
Professional Services	2.3%	0.0%	−2.3%
Transportation Infrastructure	1.8%	0.0%	−1.8%
Marine	1.6%	1.5%	−0.1%
Airlines	1.3%	9.5%	8.2%
Total	**100.0%**	**100.0%**	**0.0%**

Source: Thomson Datastream; MSCI, Inc.[8] as of 12/31/08.

underweighting those likeliest to underperform. Table 7.6 shows how you can make different portfolio bets against the benchmark by over- and underweighting industries.

Note: Portfolio A might be a portfolio of all Industrials stocks, or it can simply represent a neutral Industrials sector allocation in a larger portfolio.

The "difference" column shows the relative difference between the benchmark and Portfolio A. In this example, Portfolio A is most overweight to Construction & Engineering and Airlines and most underweight to Machinery and Road & Rail.

In other words, for this hypothetical example, Portfolio A's owner expects Construction & Engineering and Airlines to outperform the sector and Road & Rail and Machinery to underperform. But in terms of benchmark risk, Portfolio A remains fairly close to the benchmark weights, so its relative risk is quite modest. This is extremely important: By managing against a benchmark, you can make strategic choices to beat the index and are well-diversified within the sector without concentrating too heavily in a specific area.

Table 7.7 is another example of relative portfolio weighting versus the benchmark. Portfolio B is significantly underweight to Aerospace & Defense and Road & Rail and most overweight to Marine and Building Products. Because the industry weights are so different from the benchmark, Portfolio B takes on substantially more relative risk than Portfolio A.

Regardless of how your portfolio is positioned relative to the benchmark, it's important to use benchmarks to identify where your relative risks are before investing. Knowing the benchmark weights and having opinions on the future performance of each industry is a crucial step in building a portfolio designed to beat the benchmark. Should you make the correct overweight and underweight decisions, you're likelier to beat the benchmark regardless of the individual securities held within. But even if you're wrong, you'll have diversified enough not to lose your shirt.

Table 7.7   Portfolio B

Industry	MSCI World	Portfolio B	Difference
Industrial Conglomerates	19.1%	20.3%	1.2%
Machinery	15.8%	16.4%	0.6%
Aerospace & Defense	15.1%	0.0%	−15.1%
Road & Rail	11.0%	0.0%	−11.0%
Electrical Equipment	8.9%	0.0%	−8.9%
Air Freight & Logistics	5.6%	18.3%	12.7%
Construction & Engineering	5.6%	0.0%	−5.6%
Commercial Services & Supplies	4.9%	0.0%	−4.9%
Trading Companies & Distributors	4.5%	1.1%	−3.4%
Building Products	2.5%	20.3%	17.8%
Professional Services	2.3%	0.0%	−2.3%
Transportation Infrastructure	1.8%	0.0%	−1.8%
Marine	1.6%	23.6%	22.0%
Airlines	1.3%	0.0%	−1.3%
Total	**100.0%**	**100.0%**	**0.0%**

Source: Thomson Datastream; MSCI, Inc.[9] as of 12/31/08.

Chapter Recap

A more effective approach to sector analysis is "top down." A top-down investment methodology analyzes big-picture factors such as economics, politics, and sentiment to forecast which investment categories are likely to outperform the market. A key part of the process is the use of benchmarks (such as the MSCI World Industrials or S&P 500 Industrials indexes), as guidelines for building portfolios, monitoring performance, and managing risk. By analyzing portfolio drivers, we can identify which Industrials industries are most attractive and unattractive, ultimately filtering down to stock selection.

- The top-down investment methodology first identifies and analyzes high-level portfolio drivers affecting broad categories of stocks. These drivers help determine portfolio country, sector, and style weights. The same methodology can be applied to a specific sector to determine industry weights.
- Quantitative factor screening helps narrow the list of potential portfolio holdings based on characteristics such as valuations, liquidity, and solvency.
- Stock selection is the last step in the top-down process. Stock selection attempts to find companies possessing strategic attributes consistent with higher-level portfolio drivers.
- Stock selection also attempts to find companies with the greatest probability of outperforming their peers.
- It's helpful to use an Industrials benchmark as a guide when constructing a portfolio to determine your industry overweights and underweights.

8

SECURITY ANALYSIS

Now that we've covered the top-down method, let's pick some stocks. This chapter walks you through analyzing individual Industrials firms using the top-down method presented in Chapter 7. Specifically, we'll demonstrate a five-step process for analyzing firms relative to peers.

Every firm and every stock is different, and viewing them through the right lens is vital. Investors need a functional, consistent, and reusable framework for analyzing securities across the sector. While by no means comprehensive, the framework provided and the questions at this chapter's end should serve as good starting points to help identify strategic attributes and company-specific risks.

While volumes have been written about individual security analysis, a top-down investment approach de-emphasizes the importance of stock selection in a portfolio. As such, we'll talk about the basics of stock analysis for the beginner-to-intermediate investor. For a more thorough understanding of financial statement analysis, valuations, modeling, and other tools of security analysis, additional reading is suggested.

Top-Down Recap

As covered in Chapter 7, you can use the top-down method to make your biggest, most important portfolio decisions first. However, the same process applies when picking stocks, and those high-level portfolio decisions ultimately filter down to individual securities.

Step one is analyzing the broader global economy and identifying various macro "drivers" affecting entire sectors or industries. Using the drivers, you can make general allocation decisions for countries, sectors, and industries versus the given benchmark. Step two is applying quantitative screening criteria to narrow the choice set of stocks. It's not until all those decisions are made that we get to analyze individual companies, which is the third and final step.

For the rest of the chapter, we assume you have already established a benchmark, solidified portfolio themes, made industry overweight and underweight decisions, and are ready to analyze firms within a *peer group*. (A peer group is a group of stocks you'd generally expect to perform similarly because they operate in the same industry, possibly share the same geography, and have similar quantitative attributes.)

MAKE YOUR SELECTION

Security analysis is nowhere near as complicated as it may seem—but that doesn't mean it's easy. Similar to your goal in choosing industry and sector weights, you've got one basic task: spot opportunities not currently discounted into prices. Or, put differently, know something others don't. Investors should analyze firms by taking consensus expectations for a company's estimated financial results and then assessing whether it will perform below, in line with, or above those baseline expectations. Profit opportunities arise when your expectations are different and more accurate than consensus expectations. Trading on widely known information or consensus expectations adds no value to the stock-selection process. Doing so is not really different than trading on a coin flip.

The top-down method offers two ways to spot such opportunities. First, accurately predict high-level macro themes affecting an industry or group of companies—these are your portfolio drivers. Second, find firms that will benefit *most* if those high-level themes and drivers play out. This is done by finding firms with *competitive advantages* (we'll explain this concept more in a bit).

Since the majority of excess return is added in higher-level decisions in the top-down process, it's not vital to pick the "best" stocks in the universe. Rather, you want to pick stocks with a good probability of outperforming their peers. Doing so can enhance returns without jeopardizing good top-down decisions by picking risky, go-big-or-go-home stocks. Being right more often than not should create outperformance relative to the benchmark over time.

A FIVE-STEP PROCESS

Analyzing a stock against its peer group can be summarized as a five-step process:

1. Understand business and earnings drivers.
2. Identify strategic attributes.
3. Analyze fundamental and stock price performance.
4. Identify risks.
5. Analyze valuations and consensus expectations.

These five steps provide a consistent framework for analyzing firms in their peer groups. While these steps are far from a full stock analysis, they provide the basics necessary to begin making better stock selections.

Step 1: Understand Business and Earnings Drivers

The first step is to understand what the business does, how it generates its earnings, and what drives those earnings. Here are a few tips to help in the process.

- **Industry overview**. Begin any analysis with a basic understanding of the firm's industry, including its drivers and risks. You should be familiar with how current economic trends affect the industry.
- **Company description**. Obtain a business description of the company, including an understanding of the products and services within each business segment. It's always best to go directly to a company's financial statements for this. (Almost

every public firm makes their financial statements readily accessible online these days.) Browse the firm's website and financial statements/reports to gain an overview of the company and how it presents itself.

- **Corporate history**. Read the firm's history since its inception. An understanding of firm history may reveal its growth strategy or consistency with success and failure. It will also provide clues on what its true core competencies are. Ask questions like: Has it been an industry leader for decades or is it a relative newcomer? Has it switched strategies or businesses often in the past?

- **Business segments**. Break down company revenues and earnings by business segment and geography to determine how and where it makes its money. Find out what drives results in each business and geographic segment. Begin thinking how each of these business segments fits into your high-level themes.

- **Recent news/press releases**. Read all recent news about the stock, including press releases. Do a Google search and see what comes up. Look for any significant announcements regarding company operations. What is the media's opinion of the firm?

- **Markets and customers**. Identify main customers operating in the market. Determine whether the firm has any particularly large single customer or a concentrated customer base.

- **Competition**. Find the main competitors and how market share compares with other industry players. Is the industry highly segmented? Assess the industry's competitive landscape. Keep in mind the biggest competitors can sometimes lurk in different industries—sometimes even in different sectors! Get a feel for how the firm stacks up—is it an industry leader or a minor player? Does market share matter in that industry?

Step 2: Identify Strategic Attributes

After gaining a firm grasp of company operations, the next step is identifying strategic attributes consistent with higher-level portfolio themes. Also known as *competitive* or *comparative advantages*, strategic attributes are unique features that allow firms to outperform their industry or sector. Since industry peers are generally affected by the same high-level drivers, strong strategic attributes are the edge in creating superior performance. Examples of strategic attributes include:

- Consolidator
- Economic sensitivity
- First mover advantage
- Geographic diversity or advantage
- High relative market share
- Low-cost producer
- Management/business strategy
- Niche markets
- Potential takeover target
- Proprietary technologies
- Pure play
- Sales relationships/distribution
- Strong balance sheet
- Strong brand name
- Vertical integration

Strategic Attributes: Making Lemonade

How do strategic attributes help you analyze individual stocks? Consider a simple example: There are five lemonade stands of similar size, product, and quality within a city block. A scorching heat wave envelops the city, sending a rush of customers in search of lemonade. Which stand benefits most from the industry-wide surge in business? This likely depends on each stand's strategic attributes. Maybe one is a cost leader and has cheapest access to homegrown lemons. Maybe one has a geographic advantage and is located next to a basketball court full of thirsty players. Or maybe one has a superior business strategy with a "buy two, get one free" initiative that drives higher sales volume and a bigger customer base. Any of these are core strategic advantages.

Portfolio drivers help determine which kind of strategic attributes are likely to face head- or tailwinds. After all, not all strategic attributes will benefit a firm in all environments. For example, while higher operating leverage might help a firm boost earnings when an industry is booming, it would have the opposite effect in a down cycle. A pertinent example to Industrials is geographic diversity and economic sensitivity. Diverse market exposure is a key attribute when global demand is strong, but it can limit revenue growth when product demand is weaker in a major foreign market. Thus, it's essential to pick strategic attributes consistent with higher-level portfolio themes.

A strategic attribute is also only effective to the extent management recognizes and takes advantage of it. Execution is key. For example, if a firm's strategic attribute is technological expertise, it should focus its effort on research and development to maintain that edge. If its strategic attribute is low-cost production relative to its peer group, it should capitalize by potentially lowering prices or expanding production (assuming the new production is also low cost) to gain market share.

Identifying strategic attributes may require thorough research of a firm's financial statements, website, news stories, history, and discussions with customers, suppliers, competitors, or management. Don't skimp on this step—be diligent and thorough in finding strategic attributes. It may feel like an arduous task at times, but it's also among the most important steps in security selection.

Step 3: Analyze Fundamental and Stock Price Performance

Once you've gained a thorough understanding of the business, earnings drivers, and strategic attributes, the next step is analyzing firm performance both fundamentally and in the stock market.

Using the latest earnings releases and annual report, analyze company performance in recent quarters to evaluate company strength. Ask:

- What are recent revenue trends? Earnings? Margins? Which business segments are seeing rising or falling sales?
- Is the firm growing its business organically, because of acquisitions, or for some other reason?

- How sustainable is their strategy and financial results?
- Are earnings growing because of strong demand or because of cost cutting?
- Are they benefiting from tax loopholes or one-time items?
- What is management's strategy to grow the business for the future?
- What is the financial health of the company?

Not all earnings results are created equal. Understanding what drives results gives clues to what will drive future performance.

Check the company's stock chart for the last few years and try to determine what has driven performance. Explain any big up or down moves and identify any significant news events. If the stock price has trended steadily downward despite consistently beating earnings estimates, there may be a force driving the whole industry down, like expectations for weakening global machinery demand. Likewise, if the company's stock soared despite reporting tepid earnings growth or prospects, there may be some force driving the industry higher, like takeover speculation. Or stocks can simply move in sympathy with the broader market. Whatever it is, make sure you know.

After analyzing the earnings announcements of a firm and its peers (these are typically posted on the investor relations section of a firm's website every quarter), you'll begin to notice similar trends and events affecting the industry. Take note of these so you can distinguish between issues that are company-specific or industry-wide. For example, economic growth or labor scarcity often affects entire Industrials industries, but hedging policies or government spending programs may only affect specific companies.

Step 4: Identify Risks

There are two main types of risk in security analysis: stock-specific risk and systematic risk (also known as non-stock specific risk). Both can be equally important to performance.

Stock-specific risks, as the name suggests, are issues affecting the company in isolation. These are mainly risks affecting a firm's business operations or future operations. Some company-specific risks are discussed in detail in the annual reports, 10-Ks for US firms, and 20-Fs for foreign filers (found at www.sec.gov). But one can't rely solely on firms' self-identifying risk factors. You must see what analysts are saying about them and identify all risks yourself. Some examples include:

- Customer concentration
- Excessive leverage or lack of access to financing
- Executive departures
- Late SEC filings
- Limited supplier relationships
- Obsolete products
- Pending corporate actions
- Pension or benefit underfunding risk
- Poor corporate governance
- Poor operational track record
- Qualified audit opinions
- Regional, political/government risk
- Regulatory or legal—outstanding litigation
- Stock ownership concentration (insider or institutional)

Systematic risks include macroeconomic or geopolitical events out of a company's control. While the risks may affect a broad set of firms, they will have varying effects on each. Some examples include:

- Currency
- Economic activity
- End-market conditions
- Geopolitical risks
- Industry cost inflation
- Interest rates
- Labor scarcity
- Legislation and regulation
- Strained supply chain

Identifying stock-specific risks helps an investor evaluate the relative risk and reward potential of firms within a peer group. Identifying systematic risks helps you make informed decisions about which industries and countries to overweight or underweight.

If you don't feel strongly about any company in a peer group within an industry you wish to overweight, you could pick the company with the least stock-specific risk. This would help to achieve the goal of picking firms with the greatest probability of outperforming their peer group and still perform in line with your higher-level themes and drivers.

Step 5: Analyze Valuations and Consensus Expectations

Valuations can be tricky things. They *are* tools used to evaluate market sentiment and expectations for firms. They *are not* a foolproof way to see if a stock is "cheap" or "expensive." Valuations are primarily used to compare firms against their peer group (or peer average) or a company's valuation relative to its own history. As mentioned earlier, stocks move not on the expected, but on the unexpected. We aim to try and gauge what the consensus expects for a company's future performance and then assess whether that company will perform below, in line with, or above expectations.

Valuations provide little information by themselves in predicting future stock performance. Just because one company's P/E is 20 while another's is 10 doesn't mean you should buy the one at 10 because it's "cheaper." There's likely a reason why one company has a different valuation than another, including such things as strategic attributes, earnings expectations, sentiment, and stock-specific risks. The main usefulness of this exercise is explaining why company valuations differ from peers and whether this difference is justified.

There are many different valuation metrics investors use in security analysis. Some of the most popular include:

- P/E (price to earnings)
- P/FE (price to forward earnings)
- P/B (price to book)

- P/S (price to sales)
- P/CF (price to cash flow)
- DY (dividend yield)
- EV/EBITDA (enterprise value to earnings before interest, taxes, depreciation, and amortization)

Once you've compiled the valuations for a peer group, try to estimate why there are relative differences and if they're justified. Is a company's relatively low valuation due to stock-specific risk or low confidence from investors? Is the company's forward P/E relatively high because consensus is wildly optimistic about the stock? Higher valuations may be entirely justified or completely unwarranted depending on the company's individual attributes and operating conditions. Seeing valuations in this way will help to differentiate firms and spot potential opportunities or risks.

Valuations should be used in combination with previous analysis of a company's fundamentals, strategic attributes, and risks. For example, the grid below shows how an investor could combine an analysis of strategic attributions and valuations to help pick firms.

Stocks with relatively low valuations but attractive strategic attributes may be underappreciated by the market. Stocks with relatively high valuations but no discernible strategic attributes may be overvalued by the market. Either way, use valuations appropriately and in the context of a larger investment opinion about a stock, not as a panacea for true value.

		Valuation Low	Valuation High
Strategic Attributes	Relatively Attractive	Best	
	Relatively Unattractive		Worst

IMPORTANT QUESTIONS TO ASK

While this chapter's framework can be used to analyze any firm, there are additional factors specific to the Industrials sector that must be considered. The following section provides some of the most important factors and questions to consider when researching firms in the sector. Answers to these questions should help distinguish between firms within a peer group and help identify strategic attributes and stock-specific risks. While there are countless other questions and factors that could and should be asked when researching Industrials firms, these should serve as a good starting point.

Revenues and Earnings Breakdown. Most firms produce more than a single product. The more diversified the revenue, the less exposed the firm is to a fluctuation in a single product or end market. A firm's product mix will also help determine what has the greatest impact on future earnings and performance. How are the firm's revenue and earnings divided between products? How does this affect margins? How does this compare to competitors? Is it more concentrated or diversified?

Bottlenecks and Capacity Constraints. Capital goods companies are generally involved in manufacturing equipment, which requires significant capacity and a number of suppliers and components. The inability to access supplies can limit production, hurt profitability, and strain customer relations. How easy is it to access necessary supplies? How easily can the firm ramp up production if demand increases? Does the firm produce all or any of its own components? How easy or difficult is it to find qualified labor?

Geographic Breakdown and Geopolitical Risk. Where does the firm primarily sell its goods? Regional prices and product demand can vary dramatically between home and export markets. Thus, geographical diversification can both mitigate the effects of big negative changes in any one market and help spur new growth opportunities in markets where conditions are more favorable.

While a number of industries operate globally, regional markets can have different operating conditions given varying economic growth patterns, local market competition, government regulation and spending, and barriers to entry.

Distribution. Distribution channels are an important driver of corporate efficiency and operational success. The size of a distribution channel can impact local market sales, help source parts, and improve customer services and product delivery times. How large is the firm's distribution network? Does it maintain distribution relationships with other companies? Where are its distribution channels located? What is the firm's strategy toward improving its distribution network?

Production Costs. Even firms in the same industry can have highly different cost profiles. What factors are driving its production costs? Where are its production facilities located? How do margins and production costs stack up relative to peers? What is the firm's strategy to mitigate industry cost inflation? Does its plan differ from competitors? How much difficulty does the firm have passing on higher costs to its customers? If it's a low-cost producer compared to peers, does it have a strategy to take advantage of that? If it's a high-cost producer, does it have a strategy to change that?

Vertical Integration. Does the firm benefit from some degree of vertical integration (i.e., does it have the ability to handle multiple stages of the production process by itself)? Does it rely on multiple suppliers for production components? Firms with more vertical integration may be able to better mitigate cost increases during inflationary periods and help limit the likelihood of supplier component shortages.

Legislative Risks. Are there any legislative risks? These can include royalties, windfall taxes, government audits, environmental legislation, product standards, pricing, labor laws, subsidies, export taxes, tariffs, and the nationalization of assets. Emission laws and environmental standards in particular are popular topics of debate in the developed world, especially for manufacturing-intensive industries.

Regulation. How are the firm's operations affected by regulation? Does the firm currently operate in a favorable regulatory environment? How might that change? How are relations with the regulatory body or government? Firms with highly regulated assets are exposed to regulatory risks, but they may also have more stable returns.

Competition. What is the competitive landscape of the industries in which it competes? Do companies work together or always act as competitors? Does it compete against companies who have historically received special treatment or maintained significant relations with the government?

Barriers to Entry. Does the firm operate in a region or industry with significant barriers to entry? Barriers to entry may include dominant market share, customer loyalty, economies of scale and capital intensity, a concentrated industry, start-up costs, patents, predatory pricing, proprietary technology and expertise, regulatory hurdles, supplier agreements, and difficulty in obtaining environmental permits. High barriers to entry typically improve pricing power and reduce competition.

Company Strategy. Does the company compete on value, price, or both? Does it grow organically or through acquisition? Are its products differentiated or commoditized? How has the company established its competitive strategy, and how does the company expect to maintain it in the future?

Technology and Innovation. New technology and innovation, especially in the developed world, can ultimately drive customer preference. Does the firm possess any proprietary technologies or patents giving it a competitive edge or pricing power? Does it have a history of innovation? Is company success predicated upon major technological advancements or is its success driven by other means?

Brand Names. Does the firm have any brand names? How does the brand name benefit the firm? Brand name can improve pricing power and increase brand loyalty.

Market Share. Dominant market share often helps improve pricing power and brand loyalty. What is the firm's market share in each of its business segments? Does the firm maintain pricing power for its products and services? Does large market share help create economies of scale and cost savings? How does the firm expect to grow or maintain its market share moving forward? How fragmented are the consumers in its end market?

Margins. How does its margins compare to peers? Are margins growing or shrinking? Does the company hedge its input costs to limit margin compression? Has the company historically offset higher costs with higher prices? High margins in a vacuum tell you little as some industries historically hold higher margins than others, which is highly recognized and discounted by the market. Margins and similarly operating ratios (operating costs/operating revenues) are particularly important to consider for Transportation industries, where oil is a large component of operating costs. Strong economic growth bolsters top-line revenue growth for the transportation industry, but it can also help prop up the price of oil, which can negatively detract from margins and earnings. Therefore, its ability to pass costs through higher prices can be a key attribute in an environment of rising raw material prices. Transportation industries attempt to counter high oil prices in a number of ways including fuel surcharges and oil hedging.

Cash Flow Use. How is the firm spending its cash flow? How stable is cash flow over time? To what degree is it buying back shares, paying dividends, spending on capital expenditures, or paying down debt? Depending on industry conditions, investors may prefer a firm rewarding shareholders with dividends and share buybacks over taking on risky new projects. Poor use of cash flow can also lessen investor faith in management given the opportunity costs of the capital.

Balance Sheet. Many Industrials firms maintain significant leverage and debt levels due to the capital-intensive nature of their business. The inherent financial risk of this financial leverage can cause large swings in profitability and create vast differences in financial health across peers. Financially healthier firms are also considered less risky and as a result have access to cheaper debt. How much debt does the firm have? How easy is it for the firm to service that debt? Does the firm's balance sheet allow it to take on additional leverage? Do current industry conditions or new profit opportunities justify taking on new debt? Does the firm have the financial ability to make large acquisitions to fuel growth? Debt isn't necessarily a bad thing—many firms generate an excellent return on borrowed funds as long as the cost of capital is less than the return it's making. In either case, it's vital to understand the capital structure of a firm.

Chapter Recap

Security analysis is not nearly as complicated as it seems. In the top-down investment process, stocks are essentially tools used to take advantage of opportunities identified in higher-level themes. Once an attractive segment of the market is identified, we attempt to determine the firms most likely to outperform their peers by finding firms with strategic attributes. While the five-step security-selection process is just one of many ways to research firms, it is an effective framework for selecting securities within the top-down process.

Do not limit yourself to the questions provided in this chapter when researching Industrials firms—they are just some tools to help you distinguish between firms. The more questions you ask, the better your analysis will be.

- Stock selection, the third and final step in the top-down investment process, attempts to identify securities that will benefit from our high-level portfolio themes.
- Ultimately, stock selection attempts to spot opportunities not currently discounted into prices.
- To identify firms most likely to outperform their peer group, we must find firms that possess competitive advantages (aka strategic attributes).
- A five-step security-selection process can be used as a framework to research firms.
- Firms within each industry have specific characteristics and strategies separating potential winners from losers. Asking the right questions can help identify those features.

ALLOCATING YOUR "CAPITAL GOOD"

In this chapter, we'll discuss various Industrials investment strategies, including examples of how to invest throughout a market cycle. We'll also briefly cover investing based on the strength of the ultimate end market. These strategies include:

- Adding value at the industry level
- Adding value at the security level
- Adding value in an Industrials sector downturn

While the strategies presented here are by no means comprehensive, they'll provide a good starting point for constructing a portfolio that can increase your likelihood of outperforming an Industrials benchmark. They should also help spur some investment strategy ideas of your own. After all, using this framework to discover information few others have discovered yet is what investing is all about.

STRATEGY 1: ADDING VALUE AT THE INDUSTRY LEVEL

The first strategy is overweighting and underweighting Industrials industries based on your market outlook and analysis (i.e., the top-down method). Within the Industrials sector, each industry falls in and out of favor frequently—no one area outperforms consistently over the long term. Each will lead or lag depending on the market dynamics, including global and/or regional growth, end market strength, a favorable interest rate environment, and regulatory conditions.

A look at the performance of the S&P 500 Industrials industries since 1995—when the indexes first began—split into two tables (Table 9.1 and Table 9.2) because of the number of industries, illustrates the variability of returns. Calendar-year industry total returns are compared to the Industrials sector. Shaded regions highlight industry outperformance relative to the Industrials sector. Table 9.1 shows industry performance for the Capital Goods industries.

Table 9.2 includes industry total returns for the Transportation and Commercial Services & Supplies industry groups. Like Table 9.1, industry outperformance has not been concentrated in just one industry. Each industry outperformed in at least four years during the 1995 through 2008 period.

Over this 14-year period, there are a few items to note, underscoring the themes and drivers covered in this book:

1. **Aerospace & Defense** outperformed from 2004 through 2008, driven by strong global defense and commercial aerospace spending.
2. **Building Products** outperformed from 2000 through 2004, driven by the strength of the US housing market and high remodeling activity as people took advantage of the low interest rate environment.
3. **Construction & Engineering** companies outperformed from 2003 through 2005, driven by oil and gas and mining capital expenditures and government infrastructure initiatives.
4. **Industrial Conglomerates** outperformed from 1995 through 2000, driven by the strength of the US economy and demand for aircraft engines, healthcare equipment, power generation equipment, and electronics.

Table 9.1 S&P 500 Industrials Industry Total Returns

Date	Industrials	Aero. & Defense	Build. Prod.	Const. & Eng.	Elec. Equip.	Ind. Cong.	Mach.	Trad. & Dist.
1995	39.1%	65.0%	35.9%	42.1%	25.0%	39.8%	24.6%	
1996	25.1%	32.8%	19.3%	–7.3%	25.6%	39.2%	24.8%	
1997	27.0%	6.6%	25.0%	–17.4%	15.6%	43.6%	37.8%	19.8%
1998	10.9%	–4.3%	6.2%	–11.7%	1.7%	37.2%	–13.7%	–5.0%
1999	21.5%	1.7%	–21.5%	–14.5%	41.6%	44.1%	17.9%	–7.4%
2000	5.9%	25.4%	–7.0%	12.3%	20.7%	0.6%	–2.9%	–5.9%
2001	–5.7%	–17.7%	–3.1%	14.4%	–22.3%	–10.2%	8.1%	40.3%
2002	–26.3%	–5.1%	–8.1%	–32.0%	–4.8%	–40.5%	–2.4%	–3.3%
2003	32.2%	23.1%	36.5%	39.8%	43.7%	34.9%	51.0%	–6.6%
2004	18.0%	16.0%	31.2%	39.5%	14.4%	19.4%	20.4%	42.7%
2005	2.3%	15.9%	–10.5%	43.2%	10.7%	–3.8%	1.0%	8.3%
2006	13.3%	25.2%	7.3%	6.7%	19.6%	8.6%	18.4%	–0.1%
2007	12.0%	19.3%	1.0%	102.7%	26.1%	4.3%	33.8%	27.2%
2008	–39.9%	–36.5%	–40.8%	–43.5%	–38.0%	–51.5%	–45.9%	–20.9%
Avg. Ann. Return	**7.3%**	**9.3%**	**2.6%**	**6.6%**	**10.4%**	**6.8%**	**9.4%**	**5.7%**
Cumulative Return	**166.6%**	**249.0%**	**43.7%**	**145.1%**	**297.7%**	**152.8%**	**251.9%**	**95.3%**
Standard Deviation	**21.9%**	**24.4%**	**22.7%**	**38.4%**	**22.6%**	**31.0%**	**24.3%**	**20.4%**

Headings: Aero. & Defense (Aerospace & Defense), Build. Prod (Building Products), Const. & Eng. (Construction & Engineering), Elec. Equip. (Electrical Equipment), Ind. Cong. (Industrial Conglomerates), Mach. (Machinery), Trad. & Dist. (Trading Companies & Distributors).

Source: Thomson Datastream; MSCI, Inc.[1] 12/31/1994–12/31/2008.

Table 9.2 S&P 500 Industrials Industry Total Returns

Date	Industrials	Air Freight & Logistics	Airlines	Road & Rail	Commercial Services & Supplies
1995	39.1%	20.0%	46.0%	41.0%	28.4%
1996	25.1%	23.5%	9.6%	15.4%	6.7%
1997	27.0%	37.2%	68.3%	15.1%	22.0%
1998	10.9%	45.8%	-3.3%	-8.5%	0.9%
1999	21.5%	-8.0%	-0.8%	-15.4%	-2.3%
2000	5.9%	-2.4%	49.0%	6.6%	3.6%
2001	-5.7%	29.8%	-32.6%	18.6%	16.0%
2002	-26.3%	-8.0%	-38.4%	-0.6%	-25.1%
2003	32.2%	21.4%	7.4%	22.3%	37.1%
2004	18.0%	22.6%	-2.9%	25.0%	6.5%
2005	2.3%	-6.8%	-4.9%	32.7%	-2.0%
2006	13.3%	3.1%	-6.7%	15.0%	11.1%
2007	12.0%	-7.2%	-20.3%	20.3%	-12.7%
2008	-39.9%	-20.3%	-29.2%	-15.7%	-25.5%
Avg. Ann. Return	7.3%	9.0%	-1.3%	11.0%	3.1%
Cumulative Return	166.6%	236.3%	-16.5%	330.8%	53.6%
Standard Deviation	21.9%	20.2%	31.8%	17.1%	18.2%

Source: Thomson Datastream; MSCI, Inc.[2] 12/31/1994 12/31/2008.

5. **Electrical Equipment** outperformed from 2002 through 2008 as manufacturing and gross fixed investment accelerated and demand for automation equipment and power-related products increased globally.

6. **Machinery** outperformed from 2000 to 2004, driven by increasing demand for heavy trucks, construction machinery, and other industrial products as commodity prices began to rise, interest rates were favorable for investment, and global economic growth reaccelerated.

7. **Road & Rail** outperformed six of the nine years between 2000 and 2008, driven by improved pricing, increased volumes, and operating improvements.

Ultimately, your decision to overweight or underweight an industry relative to the benchmark should jive with your higher-level portfolio drivers. Based on the themes and drivers covered throughout this book, you should now have an understanding of the fundamentals driving Industrials stock returns and the tools to track them moving forward.

Using these fundamentals, some general conclusions can be made about which industries and sub-industries are more likely to perform better in different market environments. Note: *Always remember past performance is no guarantee of future performance.* The past is about understanding context and precedent for investing—it's not a roadmap for the future. Sectors are dynamic and fundamentals change over time. That said, based on industry fundamentals, here's a look at some of the reasons industries have tended to outperform or underperform historically.

Industry Cheat Sheet

Aerospace & Defense

- Defense firms tend to do well when expectations for future defense spending and military modernization efforts are rising.
- Defense companies have historically outperformed in bear markets and recessions because product demand is less variable compared to more economically sensitive industries.

(Contiuned)

- Aerospace companies tend to do well when air travel fundamentals are favorable, including sustained economic growth, increased air traffic, and airline profitability.
- Market acceptance of a new design is crucial given production and design costs and the numbers of years the planes remain in service (Boeing's 747 was first introduced in 1970 and is still flying today).
- A number of the larger US Aerospace & Defense companies reach a diversified set of markets, linking them to the broad economy as a result.

Air Freight & Logistics

- Package delivery demand tends to correlate with economic strength over time. Air Freight firms like FedEx and UPS are generally seen as barometers of the US economy and tend to do well when economic growth expectations are increasing.
- Like its transportation peers, weak economic conditions and high oil prices can challenge profitability and limit industry success.

Airlines

- The Airline industry is one of the few Industrials industries driven by consumers. Growth is driven by consumer wealth and travel demand.
- Airline travel demand is both discretionary and elastic— as a result, airline pricing can have a dramatic effect on demand, profitability, and share prices.
- Although Airlines do hedge their oil needs, rising prices can have a detrimental effect on profitability and subsequently share prices.

Building Products

- US Building Products firms tend to do well when residential and non-residential construction is strong and remodeling activity is elevated.

Construction & Engineering

- Construction & Engineering firms tend to do well when corporate and government spending on infrastructure and commercial construction is strong.
- Pay attention to major project delays and escalating project costs because this can have a significant impact on profitability.
- Global shortages of qualified engineers can cap the growth of individual firms.

Commercial Services & Supplies

- Commercial Services & Supplies firms are very diverse, but generally do well when corporate spending is high and the economy is strong.

- Environmental & Facilities Services companies tend to do well during periods of economic growth and strong construction levels, which tend to increase trash levels. Economic growth supports pricing power as well.
- The industry has tended to be more defensive than other Industrials industries.

Electrical Equipment

- Demand for electrical products historically follows general economic conditions and is generally sensitive to activity in the construction market, industrial production levels, electronic component production and spending by utilities for replacements, expansions, and efficiency improvements.
- Electrical equipment companies tend to do well when pricing increases can stay above input cost pressures.
- A slowdown in corporate profitability and a decrease in manufacturing levels can slow electrical equipment demand.

Industrial Conglomerates

- Industrial Conglomerates are exposed to many end markets and tend to do well when the global economy is strong.
- Strong infrastructure spending helps drive the larger Industrial Conglomerates that manufacture large fixed assets.
- Global diversification helps drive relative outperformance when the global economy performs better than the domestic economy.

Machinery

- Demand for machinery has historically followed general economic conditions and is generally sensitive to construction market activity, industrial production levels, commodity prices, and corporate capital expenditure trends.

Marine

- Dry bulk shipping demand is generally driven by the strength of the global economy and demand for food and commodities. Shipping rates are also driven by dry bulk demand, as well as available ship supply and port capacity, both of which are expected to increase moving forward.
- Wet bulk shipping demand is driven by demand for oil and oil derivatives like petrochemicals.
- Container ship firms are driven by global trade and available supply ships.

(Contiuncd)

Professional Services

- Professional Services firms are driven by corporate activity and consulting and legal service needs.
- Human Resource & Employment Services companies tend to be driven by employment demand and corporate profitability.

Road & Rail

- Trucking and rail companies are driven by global economic growth and consumer and corporate spending levels.
- The industry historically has been highly sensitive to oil prices and corporate success will likely be driven by how well it can pass on higher costs to its customers.
- Operational improvements play heavily on stock prices and profitability.

Trading Companies & Distributors

- US trading companies tend to be leveraged to US economic growth and industrial production and manufacturing levels, while foreign firms tend to be driven by global economic growth and commodity prices.
- Sales are driven by both corporate and government spending levels.

Transportation Infrastructure

- Transportation Infrastructure has historically been considered a defensive industry as toll-road demand is usually fairly stable.
- A decrease in road traffic is primarily driven by the macro environment and oil prices.
- Port operators tend to do well when global trade is strong. Limited global capacity magnifies the industry's sensitivity to elevated product demand.

Once you have evaluated a sector's fundamentals and formed opinions about expected returns, you need to implement industry or sub-industry allocation over- and underweights in order to:

- Determine your weights relative to a benchmark.
- Make relative over- and underweight decisions (e.g., decide what *percentage* of your portfolio should be allocated to each

industry or sub-industry) based on the conviction of your higher-level portfolio themes.

- Select stocks representative of those industries—either the biggest or with the highest correlation. Alternately, you can gain industry-level and sub-industry exposure through ETFs or low-cost mutual funds. (For more information on available ETFs, visit www.ishares.com, www.sectorspdr.com, or www .masterdata.com.)

STRATEGY 2: ADDING VALUE AT THE SECURITY LEVEL

A more advanced strategy entails investing in stocks within an industry based on a more specific and granular strategy. This could be based on different opinions about specific end markets, regions, corporate initiatives, or some combination of all the above. For example, if you think agricultural machinery manufacturers will do better than construction equipment manufacturers in the near future, you could:

1. Short construction equipment manufacturers and go long agricultural equipment manufacturers.
2. Overweight machinery producers who derive the greatest percentage of profits from the agricultural market and underweight their construction-leveraged competitors.
3. Buy machinery manufacturers with the greatest geographic exposure to agricultural areas (Midwest US, Latin America, China, etc.).
4. Overweight machinery producers with the highest correlation to agricultural commodity price changes.

These are just a few examples, but countless other tactics could be employed within Industrials industries. As you become more familiar with specific Industrials firms and their industries, you can eventually develop your own strategies. Always be vigilant for company-specific issues that could cause a stock to act differently than you would expect in the context of your broader strategy. (And be sure to revisit Chapter 8 for how to select individual stocks.)

STRATEGY 3: INDUSTRIALS SECTOR DOWNTURN

Most of this book focused on what drives the Industrials sector and its industries. But what could cause Industrials to underperform? Remember, no single sector or industry can outperform forever. The stock market eventually uncovers all opportunities for excess returns and sector leadership changes. So it's important to continually review all the drivers and question your high-level portfolio themes regularly.

A downturn in the Industrials sector could be triggered by a decline in global GDP, a fall in industrial production, and a reduction in corporate spending. While there are countless reasons why this could happen, here are a few possible examples of falling demand:

- Recession—regional or global; perceived or real
- Reduction in corporate capital expenditures
- Weakening corporate profitability
- Difficulty accessing credit to purchase new equipment
- Falling construction activity
- Commodity pressures—high prices drive commodity producer expansions but hurt manufacturers who have the commodity as an input cost
- Reduction in government infrastructure and defense spending
- Removal of government tax incentives for equipment purchases and alternative energy spending
- Inability to source necessary parts and supplies

Should your analysis lead you to believe the next 12 months will be a period of Industrials underperformance—because of the reasons previously mentioned or another driver you discover—then it may be appropriate to either reduce or eliminate your weight in Industrials firms or adopt an overall defensive position in the portfolio.

HOW TO IMPLEMENT YOUR STRATEGY

Let's briefly look at a few examples of how to implement these strategies in a portfolio. If you expect an industry to outperform relative to the benchmark and want to overweight it, you can use what you learned in Chapter 8 to pick stocks likely to outperform their peers.

But if you don't want to do that heavy of an analysis on individual stocks, you could purchase the largest stocks in the industry in an attempt to mimic it. Frequently, by owning the largest stocks you can often create a good proxy that acts very similarly to the industry's performance as a whole. For example, Caterpillar, the largest weight within the S&P 500 Machinery Index as of December 31, 2008, had a monthly correlation of 0.87 to the S&P 500 Machinery industry from 1995 through 2008.[3]

You can also use ETFs to gain broad exposure to an industry or the entire sector. For example, the iShares Dow Jones US Industrial (ticker: IYJ) and iShares S&P Global Industrials (ticker: EXI) are designed to track sector level performance. The iShares Dow Jones US Aerospace & Defense (ticker: ITA) is designed to track on an industry level, while the Market Vectors Agribusiness ETF (ticker: MOO) is meant to track all companies leveraged to a particular industry driver. (Note: These are just a few examples of securities designed to track industries. Further research should be done for more investment options. More information can be found at www.masterdata.com, which lists over 7,000 ETFs on a variety of sectors, industries, and regions.)

The smaller the industry or sub-industry, however, the less likely an ETF exists to track the exposure you desire. If using ETFs, always be sure to investigate underlying holdings to ensure they track the actual region, index, or sub-industry you want. If you are using a global index as your benchmark, a US-only Industrials ETF is unlikely to closely track the returns of the Industrials sector in your benchmark.

If you have lower expectations for the sector, you can simply underweight by selling stock or reducing your ETF weight. You can even short individual securities or ETFs in an attempt to capitalize on a sector you suspect will underperform. But shorting is a more sophisticated strategy. As are using margin or options (which can be used either to augment an over- or underweight). Because of the potential leverage involved, such strategies should only be used by sophisticated investors.

If you're outright bearish on the entire industry or stocks in general, a simple strategy is to hold cash/bonds. Keep in mind—such a strategy is far riskier than it sounds. This is seriously deviating from your benchmark, and you run the risk of being wrong and missing equity-like upside. But should you be confident in your bearish forecast, you can again short stocks or ETFs, buy reverse ETFs, and use options in an attempt to get better than cash- or bond-like returns.

For most investors, it's usually best to stick to a straightforward strategy of using ETFs and single stocks to over- and underweight industries and sub-industries based on your forecast.

Chapter Recap

We couldn't possibly list every investment strategy out there for this dynamic sector. Different strategies will work best at different times. Some will become obsolete. New ones will be discovered. Whatever strategies you choose, *always know you could be wrong!* Decisions to significantly overweight or underweight an industry relative to the benchmark, using shorting or options strategies, or speculating on commodity prices should be based on a multitude of factors, including an assessment of risk. The point of benchmarking is to properly diversify, so make sure you always have counterstrategies built into your portfolio.

- There are numerous ways to invest in the Industrials sector. These include investing in indexes or mutual funds, buying ETFs, or buying individual stocks.
- Investors can enhance returns by overweighting and underweighting Industrials industries based on a variety of high-level drivers.
- An advanced strategy involves making bets on firms with different business lines within industries like buying a Machinery firm highly leveraged to the agricultural market and shorting its competitors that focus primarily on the construction market.
- There are countless reasons Industrials could underperform including a reduction in capital expenditures and construction and manufacturing activity.

Appendix
Industrials Websites and
Data Sources

Below is a list of websites investors may find useful when monitoring and evaluating the sector. We encourage you to explore these pages and learn how the sector works in greater detail on your own. The Industrials websites and data sources below have been broken down into three sections—forecasts/annual reports, data providers, and news sources. Websites are generally only listed once, but they often include information from the other two categories.

Forecasts/Annual Reports

Aerospace Industries Association Forecast	www.aia-aerospace.org/industry_information/economics/year_end_review_and_forecast
AIA Construction Forecast	www.aia.org/econ_constforecast
Annual Construction Equipment Business Outlook	www.aem.org/Trends/Reports/IndustriesOutlook
Current Market Outlook (Commercial Boeing)	www.boeing.com/commercial/cmo
FAA Aerospace Forecast	www.faa.gov/data_statistics/aviation/aerospace_forecasts
International Air Traffic Association Industry Outlook	www.iata.org/whatwedo/economics/industry_outlook.htm
ISM Manufacturing Report on Business	www.ism.ws/ISMReport/SemiannualIndex.cfm
USDA Agricultural Projections	www.ers.usda.gov/publications/oce081

Data

Bureau of Economic Analysis	www.bea.gov
Bureau of Transportation Statistics	www.bts.gov/programs/freight_transportation
Cass Information Systems Freight Index	www.cassinfo.com
Census Bureau	www.census.gov
Department of Defense	www.defenselink.ml
Electroindustry Business Confidence Indices	www.nema.org/econ/ebci
Equipment Leasing and Finance Association (ELFA)	http://www.elfaonline.org/
Federal Reserve	www.federalreserve.org
Global Manufacturing & Services PMI	www.ism.ws
IMF	www.imf.org
Institute of Supply Management	www.ism.ws
OECD	www.oecd.org
Robotic Industries Association	www.robotics.org
United Nations	www.un.org
World Bank	www.worldbank.org
World Trade Organization	www.wto.org

News

Air Cargo World	www.aircargoworld.com
Air Transport Association	www.airlines.org
Association of Equipment Manufacturers	www.aem.org/News
Aviation Week	www.aviationweek.com
Construction Equipment	www.newsletters.agc.org/datadigest
Defense News	www.defensenews.com
Dry Bulk Index	www.drybulkindex.com
Industrial Market Trends	news.thomasnet.com/IMT/index.html
Industry Week	www.industryweek.com
Logistics Management	www.logisticsmgmt.com
Manufacturing Economy Daily	www.nam.org
MAPI Manufacturing	www.mapi.net
McGraw Hill Construction	www.construction.com
Quadrennial Defense Report	www.defenselink.mil/qdr
Railway Age	www.railwayage.com/index.html
Supply Chain Brain	www.supplychainbrain.com
Traffic World	www.trafficworld.com
Transport Topics	www.ttnews.com

Notes

CHAPTER 1: INDUSTRIALS SECTOR BASICS

1. Bloomberg Finance L.P.
2. Ibid.
3. Ibid.
4. Securities and Exchange Commission, AMR Corporation Form 10-K, http://idea.sec.gov/Archives/edgar/data/6201/000000620109000009/ar120810k.htm?bcsi_scan_408DE456E3075246=0&bcsi_scan_filename=ar120810k.htm (accessed February 19, 2009).
5. Ibid.
6. James P. Womack, Daniel T. Jones, and Daniel Roos, *The Machine that Changed the World*, (Harper Perennial: 1990).
7. Ibid.
8. Michael Marx, "Sigma Saves Fortune 500 $427 Billion," *Market Wire* (January 11, 2007), http://www.marketwire.com/press-release/Isixsigma-Llc-717313.html (accessed February 3, 2009).
9. Motorola, Inc, "About Motorola University," http://www.motorola.com/content.jsp?globalObjectId=3081 (accessed February 19, 2009).
10. General Electric, "GE 1999 Annual Report Letter to Share Owners," http://www.ge.com/annual99/letter/letter_three.html (accessed March 16, 2009).

CHAPTER 2: HISTORY OF MODERN MANUFACTURING

1. General Electric Share Owners Letter, http://www.ge.com/annual00/letter/index.html (accessed February 4, 2009).
2. Securities and Exchange Commission, "2007 General Electric Form 10–K," http://idea.sec.gov/Archives/edgar/data/40545/000004054508000011/frm10k.htm (accessed February 4, 2009).

3. US Department of Transportation, "The Changing Face of Transportation," Bureau of Transportation Statistics, http://www .bts.gov/publications/the_changing_face_of_transportation/chapter_ 04.html (accessed February 4, 2009).

4. Securities and Exchange Commission, Emerson Electric Form 10–K, http://idea.sec.gov/Archives/edgar/data/32604/000114420408066523/ v132847_10k.htm; US Securities and Exchange Commission, Ingersoll Rand Form 10–K, http://idea.sec.gov/Archives/edgar/data/1160497/00 0119312509042566/d10k.htm (accessed February 3, 2009).

5. George Ritzer, *The Blackwell Companion to Globalization* (Wiley-Blackwell: September 2007).

6. Ibid.

7. Paul Knox and John Agnew, *The Geography of the World Economy* (Hodder Arnold: 1998).

8. Chalmers Johnson, *MITI and the Japanese Miracle: The Growth of Industrial Policy, 1925–1975,* (Stanford University Press: 1982). *Growth* rate calculated using manufacturing indices.

9. WT Beasley, *The Rise of Modern Japan* (St. Martin's Press, Inc: 1990).

10. Andrew Gordon, *A Modern History of Japan* (Oxford University Press: 2003).

11. See note 7.

12. Edwin O. Reischauer, *Japan: The Story of a Nation* (McGraw-Hill: 1989).

13. Patricia Panchak, "Shaping the Future of Manufacturing," *Industry Week* (January 1, 2005), http://www.industryweek.com/ReadArticle. aspx?ArticleID=9524 (accessed February 4, 2009).

14. Jim Rowher, *Asia Rising Why America Will Prosper as Asia's Economies Boom* (Simon & Schuster: 1995).

15. Ibid.

16. Frank B. Tipton, *The Rise of Asia: Economy, Society, and Politics in Contemporary Asia* (University of Hawaii Press: 1998).

17. Ibid.

18. The World Bank, *The East Asian Miracle: Economic Growth and Public Policy* (Oxford University Press: 1993).

19. United Nations Conference on Trade and Development, "Inward FDI Performance Index—Results for 2005–2007," http://www.unctad.org/ Templates/WebFlyer.asp?intItemID=2471&lang=1 (accessed February 4, 2009).

20. Eswar Prasad, "China's Growth and Integration into the World Economy: Prospects and Challenges," International Monetary Fund (2004), http://www.imf.org/external/pubs/ft/op/232/op232.pdf (accessed February 4, 2009).

21. "China Ranks 2nd with 8.8% of World's Exports by 2007," *China View* (October 28, 2008), http://news.xinhuanet.com/english/2008-10/28/content_10266111.htm (accessed February 4, 2009).

22. George Church, "1985 Person of the Year—Deng Xiaoping," *Time Magazine,* January 6, 1986.

23. Ibid.

24. See note 19.

25. The World Bank, *Big Dragon, Little Dragons: China's Challenge to the Machinery Exports of Southeast Asia* (World Bank: 2007).

26. Mary Amiti and Caroline Freund, *The Anatomy of China's Export Growth* (World Bank: 2008).

27. "Classification and Statistical Reconciliation of Trade in Advanced Technology Products: The Case of China and the United States," Brookings Institute (Spring 2008), http://www.brookings.edu/papers/2008/spring_china_btc.aspx (accessed February 4, 2009).

28. William Strauss, "Is the US Losing Its Manufacturing Hub? *Swiss Business Hub*" (October 2, 2007), http://www.swissbusinesshub.com/photos/news/Presentation_02_William_Strauss.ppt (accessed February 4, 2009).

29. US Federal Reserve; Bureau of Economic Analysis.

CHAPTER 3: INDUSTRIALS SECTOR DRIVERS

1. Securities and Exchange Commission, Boeing Company Form 10–K

2. The Associated Press, "Hope for Progress in Arms Control," *International Herald Tribune* (June 9, 2008), http://www.iht.com/articles/2008/06/09/europe/arms.php (accessed February 3, 2009).

CHAPTER 4: INDUSTRIALS SECTOR BREAKDOWN

1. Source: MSCI. The MSCI information may only be used for your internal use, may not be reproduced or redisseminated in any form and may not be used to create any financial instruments or products or any indices. The MSCI information is provided on an "as is" basis and the user of this information assumes the entire risk of any use made of this

information. MSCI, each of its affiliates and each other person involved in or related to compiling, computing or creating any MSCI information (collectively, the "MSCI Parties") expressly disclaims all warranties (including, without limitation, any warranties of originality, accuracy, completeness, timeliness, non-infringement, merchantability and fitness for a particular purpose) with respect to this information. Without limiting any of the foregoing, in no event shall any MSCI Party have any liability for any direct, indirect, special, incidental, punitive, consequential (including, without limitation, lost profits) or any other damages.

2. Ibid.

3. Ibid.

4. Ibid.

5. Currency conversions for non-US firms calculated using prevailing rates at the end of each firm's fiscal year.

6. Securities and Exchange Commission, "Lockheed Martin Annual Report," http://www.sec.gov/Archives/edgar/data/936468/00011931250 8041793/d10k.htm#tx41459_3 (accessed February 5, 2009).

7. Securities and Exchange Commission, "Raytheon Company Form 10–K," http://www.sec.gov/Archives/edgar/data/1047122/0001193125 08039853/d10k.htm?bcsi_scan_408DE456E3075246=0&bcsi_scan_ filename=d10k.htm (accessed February 5, 2009).

8. Securities and Exchange Commission, "Boeing Company Form 10–K," http://www.sec.gov/Archives/edgar/data/12927/000119312508032328 /d10k.htm (accessed February 5, 2009).

9. Boeing Current Market Outlook 2008–2027.

10. Securities and Exchange Commission, "Masco Form 10–K," http:// www.sec.gov/Archives/edgar/data/62996/00009501240800079 2/k22937e10vk.htm (accessed February 5, 2009); Securities and Exchange Commission, "USG Corp Form 10–K," http://www .sec.gov/Archives/edgar/data/757011/0000950137080023386/ c23836e10vk.htm (accessed February 5, 2009).

11. Securities and Exchange Commissions, "Armstrong World Form 10–K," http://www.sec.gov/Archives/edgar/data/7431/0001193125080426 94/ d10k.htm (accessed February 5, 2009).

12. American Society of Civil Engineers, "2009 Report Card for America's Infrastructure," http://www.asce.org/reportcard/2009/ (accessed February 5, 2009).

13. Bloomberg Finance LP, data accessed on 02/04/2009, includes partial acquisition.

14. Bureau of Economic Analysis, "Table 5.5.5 Private Fixed Investment in Equipment and Software by Type," US Department of Economic Analysis (August 6, 2008), http://bea.gov/national/nipaweb/TableView. asp?SelectedTable=146&Freq=Year&FirstYear=2006&LastYear=2007 (accessed February 5, 2009).

15. Securities and Exchanges Commission, "Caterpillar Form 10–K," http://www.sec.gov/Archives/edgar/data/18230/000001823008000052 /form10k_2007.htm (accessed February 5, 2009).

16. "Investor Presentation," United Rentals (November 2008), http://www. ur.com/files/website/live/investor/presentations/URINV_Nov08.pdf (accessed February 5, 2009).

17. Securities and Exchange Commission, "Parker-Hannifan Form 10–K," http://sec.gov/Archives/edgar/data/76334/000119312507191627/ d10k.htm (accessed February 5, 2009).

18. Securities and Exchange Commission, "Fastenal Form 10–K," http:// www.sec.gov/Archives/edgar/data/815556/000119312508035349/ d10k.htm (accessed February 5, 2009).

19. Air Transport Association, "2008 Economic Report," www.airlines. org/NR/rdonlyres/770B5715-5C6F-44AA-AA8C-DC9AEB4E7E12/0/ 2008AnnualReport.pdf (accessed February 5, 2009).

20. Securities and Exchange Commission, "Ryder Systems 2007 Form 10–K," (February 12, 2008), http://www.sec.gov/Archives/edgar/data/ 85961/000095014408000905/g11625e10vk.htm (accessed February 5, 2009).

21. Securities and Exchange Commission, "Kirby Corporation Form 10–K," (February 27, 2008), http://www.sec.gov/Archives/edgar/ data/56047/000095012908001244/h53780e10vk.htm?bcsi_scan_ 408DE456E3075246=0&bcsi_scan_filename=h53780e10vk.htm (accessed February 5, 2009).

22. Securities and Exchange Commissions, "Werner Form 10–K," http:// www.sec.gov/Archives/edgar/data/793074/000079307408000069/ wern10k2007.txt (accessed February 5, 2009).

23. American Association of Railroads, "Overview of America's Freight Railroads," (May 2008), www.aar.org/PubCommon/Documents/About TheIndustry/Overview.pdf (accessed February 5, 2009).

CHAPTER 5: STAYING CURRENT: TRACKING SECTOR FUNDAMENTALS

1. Securities and Exchange Commission, "CNH Global 2007 Form 20–F," http://idea.sec.gov/Archives/edgar/data/1024519/000119312508046688/d20f.htm (accessed February 4, 2009).
2. Equipment Leasing and Finance Association, "Monthly Leasing and Finance Index," (January 2009), http://www.elfaonline.org/ind/research/MLFI/1208.cfm (accessed March 16, 2009).
3. Caterpillar, "2007 Monthly Dealer Statistics," (January 25, 2008), http://www.cat.com/cda/files/778358/7/Archeive2007.pdf (accessed February 4, 2009).

CHAPTER 6: THE INFRASTRUCTURE MARKET

1. Terex 1Q08 Earnings Conference Call, Seeking Alpha, http://seekingalpha.com/article/73866-terex-corp-q1-2008-earnings-call-transcript?page=-1) (accessed February 4, 2009).
2. Marianne Fay and Tito Yepes, "Investing in Infrastructure: What is Needed from 2000 to 2010?" (July 17, 2003), World Bank Policy Research, http://ssrn.com/abstract=636464 (accessed February 4, 2009).
3. Ibid.
4. Infrastructure to 2030 (Volume 2): Mapping Policy for Electricity, Water and Transport, OECD (2007), http://www.oecd.org/document/49/0,3343,en_2649_36240452_38429809_1_1_1_1,00.html (accessed February 4, 2009).
5. Morgan Stanley, "Emerging Markets Infrastructure: Just Getting Started," (April 2008), www.morganstanley.com/views/perspectives/files/infrastructure_paper4.pdf (accessed February 4, 2009).
6. Canwest News Service, "Canada's Crumbling Infrastructure Reaching Critical," (August 21, 2008), http://www.canada.com/ottawacitizen/news/story.html?id=1275e78d-18bd-4c25-86e9-1c9f3389f2c4.
7. American Society of Civil Engineers "2009 Report Card for America's Infrastructure," http://www.asce.org/reportcard/2009/ (accessed February 5, 2009).
8. Kevin Hamlin, "China's Spending May Thwart Olympic Curse, Buoy Asia," Bloomberg (September 1, 2008), http://www.bloomberg.com/apps/news?pid=20601109&sid=a0MhO00B.Zto&refer=home (accessed February 5, 2009).

9. "National Infrastructure Program 2007–2012," Mexican Government, www.infraestructura.gob.mx/pdf/NationalInfrastructureProgram2007-2012.pdf (accessed February 5, 2009).

10. Maria Levitov, "Putin to Spend Record on Russian Transport System," Bloomberg (May 20, 2008), http://www.bloomberg.com/apps/news?pid=20601095&refer=east_europe&sid=aL8tv7Q8ENdw (accessed February 5, 2009).

11. Dylan Bowman, "$800bn Investment in Saudi Over Next 10 years," *Arabian Business* (September 15, 2008), http://www.arabianbusiness.com/531076-800bn-investment-in-saudi-over-ncxt-10-years (accessed February 5, 2009).

12. "Brazil to Raise Investment Spending to Spark Growth," Bloomberg (February 4, 2009), http://www.bloomberg.com/apps/news?pid=10000086&refer=latin_America&sid=aTHxP0ox8qEM (accessed February 5, 2009).

13. American Society of Civil Engineers, "2005 Report Card for America's Infrastructure," http://www.asce.org/reportcard/2005/page.cfm?id=203 (accessed February 5, 2009).

14. Joy Global Earnings Call Transcript, March 23, 2008.

15. Michael Porter and Klaus Schwab, "The Global Competitiveness Report 2008–2009," World Economic Forum, http://www.weforum.org/pdf/GCR08/GCR08.pdf (accessed February 5, 2009).

16. Paul Simao, "Soccer-Cost of 2010 World Cup Stadiums Hit by Weak Rand," Reuters UK (December 10, 2008), http://uk.reuters.com/article/worldFootballNews/idUKLA57408820081210 (accessed February 5, 2009); Mike Cohen, "South Africa Says World Cup Stadiums to Exceed Budget," Bloomberg (August 13, 2008), http://www.bloomberg.com/apps/news?pid=20601116&sid=aPQvTMt2xfAc&refer=africa (accessed February 5, 2009); Bheki Mpofu, "World Cup Cities to be Asked to Chip In," *Business Day* (August 14, 2008), http://www.businessday.co.za/articles/topstories.aspx?ID=BD4A822022 (accessed February 5, 2009).

CHAPTER 7: THE TOP-DOWN METHOD

1. Matthew Kalman, "Einstein Letters Reveal a Turmoil Beyond Science," Boston Globe (July 11, 2006), http://www.boston.com/news/world/middleeast/articles/2006/07/11/einstein_letters_reveal_a_turmoil_beyond_science/ (accessed May 9, 2008).

2. Michael Michalko, "Combinatory Play," Creative Thinking, http://www.creativethinking.net/DT10_CombinatoryPlay.htm?Entry=Good (accessed May 9, 2008).

3. Gary P. Brinson, Brian D. Singer, and Gilbert L. Beebower, "Determinants of Portfolio Performance II: An Update." *The Financial Analysts Journal 47* (1991 [3]): 40–48.

4. Source: MSCI. The MSCI information may only be used for your internal use, may not be reproduced or redisseminated in any form and may not be used to create any financial instruments or products or any indices. The MSCI information is provided on an "as is" basis and the user of this information assumes the entire risk of any use made of this information. MSCI, each of its affiliates and each other person involved in or related to compiling, computing or creating any MSCI information (collectively, the "MSCI Parties") expressly disclaims all warranties (including, without limitation, any warranties of originality, accuracy, completeness, timeliness, non-infringement, merchantability and fitness for a particular purpose) with respect to this information. Without limiting any of the foregoing, in no event shall any MSCI Party have any liability for any direct, indirect, special, incidental, punitive, consequential (including, without limitation, lost profits) or any other damages.

5. Ibid.

6. Ibid.

7. Ibid.

8. Ibid.

9. Ibid.

CHAPTER 9: ALLOCATING YOUR "CAPITAL GOOD"

1. Source: MSCI. The MSCI information may only be used for your internal use, may not be reproduced or redisseminated in any form and may not be used to create any financial instruments or products or any indices. The MSCI information is provided on an "as is" basis and the user of this information assumes the entire risk of any use made of this information. MSCI, each of its affiliates and each other person involved in or related to compiling, computing or creating any MSCI information (collectively, the "MSCI Parties") expressly disclaims all warranties (including, without limitation, any warranties of originality, accuracy,

completeness, timeliness, non-infringement, merchantability and fitness for a particular purpose) with respect to this information. Without limiting any of the foregoing, in no event shall any MSCI Party have any liability for any direct, indirect, special, incidental, punitive, consequential (including, without limitation, lost profits) or any other damages.

2. Ibid.
3. Thomson Datastream.

Glossary

Aftermarket Non-factory products, accessories, and services to replace, repair, or overhaul original equipment.

Available seat mile (ASM) Number of seats available to purchase, multiplied by the number of miles flown. ASM is a measure of airline capacity.

Backlog Orders that have been received and have to be fulfilled.

Baltic Dry Freight Index A shipping index that measures the cost to transport raw materials. The index, compiled by the Baltic Exchange, is a composite of prices for shipping dry commodities around the world.

Budget appropriations The actual funding levels for a project for a particular year. This is primarily seen when analyzing the defense budget.

Budget authorizations The total amount that can be spent in aggregate on a particular project over its life. This is primarily seen when analyzing the defense budget.

Class I railroads The largest North American railroads that meet predefined revenue criteria.

Containerization Shipping method where goods are packaged in large standardized containers.

Cost-plus contracts Contractors are paid a fee for their services and are reimbursed for their allowable costs.

Dead-weight ton Measure of how much weight a ship can carry.

Double-stack Stacking one rail car container on top of another to double a train's capacity.

Dwell time The amount of time a train is docked at the station.

Earth-moving machine Machines used in civil engineering and construction projects, including excavators, cranes, and bulldozers.

Excavators Construction machinery used for multiple purposes including excavating, digging, and material loading.

Fixed-price contract A negotiated contract in which a contractor is given a fixed sum for completing a contract. Profit is generated when actual costs are less than the costs to complete the contract.

Full truckload Freight shipments where a full truck is utilized by one shipper and shipments go to one place.

Funded backlog Uncompleted firm orders for which funding has been both authorized and appropriated.

Heavy construction equipment Construction equipment weighing over 12 metric tons, usually used in infrastructure projects and mining applications.

Horizontal keiretsu A Japanese corporate organizational structure where a family of firms cooperate and often take equity stakes in each other. A bank & trading company are usually in the center.

HVAC Heating, ventilation, and air conditioning equipment.

Hydraulic machinery Machines and tools powered by liquid, often oil-based, which is controlled by valves. This includes pumps, motors, and cylinders.

Intermodal transport Shipments where more than one mode of transportation is utilized (e.g., shipments via railroad and truck).

Inventory Values of raw materials and supplies purchased for use in production and finished products not yet sold.

Large commercial aircraft Commercial airplanes that seat more than 110 people.

Less-than-truckload Freight shipment where a truck is shared among multiple customers, with shipments typically weighing 10,000 pounds or less.

Light construction equipment Construction equipment weighing under 12 metric tons, usually used in residential and commercial construction.

Operating ratio Total operating costs divided by revenues. The operating ratio is used most commonly in transportation industries as a measure of operating efficiency.

Passenger load factor The proportion of aircraft seating capacity to seats sold and utilized.

Pneumatic machine Machines that are powered by compressed air or gas.

Regional aircraft Commercial airplanes that seat 110 people or less.

Revenue passenger miles (RPM) Total number of passengers paying revenue, multiplied by the total distance traveled. RPM reflects the number of available seats actually sold.

Terminal dwell time Time a rail car spends at its terminal.

Time-and-materials contracts Contracts under which contractors are paid an hourly rate for labor and reimbursed for allowable direct costs.

Twenty-foot equivalent units (TEU) Standard unit of shipping container capacity, equal to one standard 20 ft (length) $\times$ 8 ft (width) container.

Unfunded backlog Uncompleted orders for which funding has not been appropriated.

Vertical keiretsu A Japanese corporate organizational structure with a major manufacturer at its core and its suppliers working closely alongside.

About the Authors

Matt C. Schrader (San Francisco, California) is an Industrials analyst for Fisher Investments. Matt graduated from the University of California at San Diego with a BS in Management Science. Matt grew up in Marin County, California, and currently resides in San Francisco.

Andrew S. Teufel (San Francisco, California) has been with Fisher Investments since 1995 where he currently serves as a Co-President and Director of Research. Prior to joining Fisher, he worked at Bear Stearns as a Corporate Finance Analyst in its Global Technology Group. Andrew also instructs at many seminar and educational workshops throughout the US and UK and lectures at the Haas School of Business at UC Berkeley. He is also the Editor-in-Chief of MarketMinder.com. Andrew is a graduate of UC Berkeley.

Index